HIS BELOVED BRIDE

His Beloved Bride: A Journey into Deeper Intimacy with Jesus

Copyright © 2019 Sula Skiles

ISBN: 9781797476858

*Cover Art by Screen Gualtieri

www.screengualtieri.com

A Publication of Tall Pine Books | tallpinebooks.com

HIS BELOVED BRIDE

A Journey Into Deeper Intimacy with Jesus

SULA SKILES

Tall Pine

ENDORSEMENTS

"Sula Skiles is a treasure in the Body of Christ. Her desire to know God in His fullness will both challenge you and stir you with a hunger to experience more of His heart. Reminiscent of Madame Guyon, she reveals an inventive life of deep romance with the Bridegroom through prose like, "Do you know what I went through just to be able to kiss you?" Her stories captivate as they draw you into a relationship with Jesus that one could only tell if they have tasted of his sweet intimacy. We were created for encounters with the Bridegroom and, as the Bride, we are the masterpiece of all creation. The world is the setting for the Bridegroom to woo His Bride and for the Bride to fall madly in love with her Husband. His Beloved Bride is a story of love. In reading it, you'll find your place in His love story."

—**DAVID & ALLESSIA EDWARDS**, Founders of *Revivalism*, Directors of *School of Revivalists*, Authors of *Revivals and Revivalists*, **revivalism.net**

"My beautiful friend Sula has written a book that will stir a hunger deep within you to passionately pursue intimacy with your Bridegroom, Jesus Christ. She unveils a truth that is vital to the modern church and her health and strength as the Bride of Christ. If you desire deeper connection to the Father this book will usher you into just that. Sula is releasing a clarion call to the church to rise to her position as the Bride and fall into the arms of her Bridegroom. This call positions us to supernaturally walk out our destiny on this earth reaching the lost and sick and dying world around us, in our day to day living. As you read you will feel the presence of the Living God surrounding you as His arms wrap tightly around you. You were made for this! Awaken, awaken to your beautiful position as Jesus' beloved bride.

—**KRISSY NELSON**, Author, Speaker, TV Host of *Created for the Impossible,* **krissynelson.com**

"This book is an invitation that unveils the revelatory depths of God. It takes you into a throne room experience that will produce a breakthrough of intimacy to come forth in your own personal walk with Jesus."

—**GINA LA MORTE**, Prophetic Seer, Author and Scribe, **GinaLaMorte.com**

CONTENTS

FOREWORD

In this book, you are going to be taken down the most valuable journey in life that you could ever possibly discover by my dear friend Sula Skiles. Both Sula and her incredible husband John are some of the most genuine Jesus lovers I know that simultaneously display God's Presence and Power to the nations of the world with a fullness like very few walk in. This book written by Sula is going to transform your life forever and literally brand your very being with the residue of heaven.

One of my favorite things about Sula is that she does not just do things to merely accomplish the next task, but she walks under specific assignments of heaven. That's what this book is. You are going to find that this writing has the literal Breath of Life upon it, bringing the very impartation of what Sula not only walks in but is carrying in such a potent way. This book is a *now and forever* Word from Heaven.

Be warned that you will never look at Jesus the same without your heart racing through the substance of He who is Love from the encounter that is in this very manuscript before you. Your ears will hear and your eyes will see at unprecedented levels as you open your heart to what the Holy Spirit is clearly conveying through Sula.

May His Bride arise at the union of one giving all Glory to Him who is comparable to none.

"But the one who joins himself to the Lord is mingled into one spirit with him." (1 Corinthians 6:17 TPT)

"Marriage is the beautiful design of the Almighty, a great and sacred mystery— meant to be a vivid example of Christ and his church." (Ephesians 5:32 TPT)

—**BRIAN GUERIN**, Founding President of *Bridal Glory International*
BridalGlory.com

Chapter One

FINDING A BRIDE FOR HIS SON

*W*hat if this world was created so that Father God could find a Bride for His Son? We get a glimpse into His purpose by looking at the end of the story: the final exclamation of the Bible is the Bride of Christ ascending into an eternal heaven to experience His love forever. It's a beautiful image.

The theme of marriage between Husband and Bride is all throughout the Bible, if only we had eyes to see. It's a theme that God has been stirring in my heart as He has invited me to closer intimacy with Him.

Loved by the Bridegroom

Years ago, the Lord started speaking to me about being His Bride. Initially, I retained the Scriptures as head knowledge. Then I started having Bridal Encounters with the Lord. Everything I learned became a deeper and deeper identity from which I began to live. I never knew that I could be loved in this way.

Over the years, I have discovered that there is so much more to experience with Jesus as the Bridegroom King Lover. It is one thing to hear about Jesus being your Husband, to learn and study the topic, but there is an invitation for believers—men *and* women—to live from this reality. He wants us to experience what it really feels like to be His Beloved Bride. It is the deepest place of intimacy and the highest place of authority.

It will be challenging to explain the fullness of this place with Him, because so much of it is unexplainable and can only be imparted through personal encounters and relationship with Jesus. In this book, I will do my best to "prepare the Bride," which is one of the greatest gifts that I could ever offer my first love, Jesus.

"'Let us be glad and rejoice, and let us give honor to Him. For the time has come for the wedding feast of the Lamb, and His bride has prepared herself. She has been given the finest of pure white linen to wear.' For the fine linen represents the good deeds of God's holy people. And the angel said to me, 'Write this: Blessed are those who are invited to the wedding feast of the Lamb.' And he added, 'These are true words that come from God.'" (Revelation 19:7-9 NLT)

The Invitation to Come

As mentioned above, the end of the story of the Bible, the end of our lives here on earth, is only the beginning of a wedding celebration with the Eternal King. We are His Bride!

Heaven rejoices over a Bride who has prepared herself. This marriage is the vision for our existence with the Lord. Are you ready? Do you yearn for Him?

"'Come,' says the Holy Spirit and the Bride in divine duet. Let everyone who hears this duet join them in saying, 'Come.' Let everyone gripped with spiritual thirst say, 'Come.' And let everyone who craves the gift of living water come and drink it freely. 'It is my gift to you! Come.'" (Revelation 22:17 TPT)

Wow, the Scriptures are so full of life and invitation. The Spirit and the Bride say "Come." Accept the invitation and drink deeply of His love.

Adopted and Engaged

Father God loves the world so much that He sent His Son so that we could enter into a family relationship with Him. We are adopted into this family through Holy Spirit. We are now children of God, His sons and daughters!

"And you did not receive the "spirit of religious duty," leading you back into the fear of never being good enough. But you have received the "Spirit of full acceptance," enfolding you into the family of God. And you will never feel orphaned, for as he rises up within us, our spirits join him in saying the words of tender affection, "Beloved Father!"

For the Holy Spirit makes God's fatherhood real to us as he whispers into our innermost being, "You are God's beloved child!" And since we are his true children, we qualify to share all his treasures, for indeed, we are heirs of God himself. And since we are joined to Christ, we also inherit all that he is and all that he has. We will experience being co-glorified with him provided that we accept his sufferings as our own." (Romans 8:15-17 TPT)

By the same Holy Spirit, our engagement to Jesus in the Bridal covenant is sealed. We are adopted and married into the family of God. Holy Spirit is like an engagement ring which validates our intimate devotion to our Bridegroom King Lover.

"Now we have been stamped with the seal of the promised Holy Spirit. He is given to us like an engagement ring is given to a bride, as the first installment of what's coming! He is our hope-promise of a future inheritance which seals us until we have all of redemption's promises and experience complete freedom—all for the supreme glory and honor of God!" (Ephesians 1:13b-14 TPT)

The Wedding Feast

Let's look at the words of our Groom Jesus and what He continually spoke of during His ministry on the earth. Jesus spoke much about the reality of the Kingdom that He came to establish. His parables and stories were to explain how His Heavenly Kingdom Realm operates.

Below, Jesus speaks of the mystery of the wedding celebration that Father God set up for Him and His Bride:

"He illustrated the reality of heaven's kingdom realm by saying, 'There once was a king who arranged an extravagant wedding feast for his son. On the day the festivities were set to begin, he sent his servants to summon all the invited guests, but they chose not to come. So the king sent even more servants to inform the invited guests, saying, "Come, for the sumptuous feast is now ready! The oxen and fattened cattle have been killed and everything is prepared, so come! Come to the wedding feast for my son and his bride!"

But the invited guests were not impressed. One was preoccupied with his business; another went off to his farming enterprise. And the rest seized the king's messengers and shamefully mistreated them, and even killed them. This infuriated the king!

So he sent his soldiers to execute those murderers and had their city burned to the ground. Then the king said to his servants, "The wedding feast is ready, yet those who had been invited to attend didn't deserve the honor. Now I want you to go into the streets and alleyways and invite anyone and everyone you find to come and enjoy the wedding feast in honor of my son." So the servants went out into the city streets and invited everyone to come to the wedding feast, good and bad alike, until the banquet hall was crammed with people! Now, when the king entered the banquet hall, he looked with glee over all his guests. But then he noticed a guest who was not wearing the wedding robe provided for him.

So he said, "My friend, how is it that you're here and you're not wearing your wedding garment?" But the man was speechless. Then the king turned to his servants and said, "Tie him up and throw him into the outer darkness, where there will be great sorrow, with weeping and grinding of teeth." For everyone is invited to enter in, but few respond in excellence.'" (Matthew 22:2-14 TPT)

Today, the Father is sending you an invitation to the wedding celebration of His Son Jesus—not just to attend as a guest, but to marry His Son! Yet we know our own sins and unrighteousness. How could we possibly marry our Bridegroom? Father God helps us get ready. Through Jesus, we are given robes of righteousness. He paid for our purity with His blood. We come into Bridal union with Him as we are made pure and wear His righteousness and not our own.

Can you see the beautiful mystery illustrated in the parable? Father God wants a Bride for His Son—and He chose us!

"I am overwhelmed with joy in the Lord my God! For he has dressed me with the clothing of salvation and draped me in a robe of righteousness. I am like a bridegroom dressed for his wedding or a bride with her jewels." (Isaiah 61:10 NLT)

Personal Encounter:

In February of 2018, I had a glorious encounter with Father God. I felt His overwhelming love and knew that He wanted to show me something through His heart. I saw a vision of a poised beautiful Bride whose face was slightly turned away. For a split second, I felt the longing of the Father to see the Bride face-to-face with the Groom.

I received revelation that many in the body of Christ don't recognize Jesus when He comes into the room, either from the busyness of the world or the blinders of religion. It's just like the religious leaders of the day who did not recognize the Lord as He walked amongst them. This encounter hurled me into a travail of intercession for the Bride. For hours, I was transfixed in that state of prayer and weighty glory. I knew Father God was placing a mandate on my life to do something about this: to turn the face of the Bride in alignment with the Bridegroom and Heaven.

"He came to the very people he created—to those who should have recognized him, but they did not receive him. But those who embraced him and took hold of his name were given authority to become the children of God!" (John 1:11-12 TPT)

Activation Prayer:

Father God, I thank You for adopting me into Your Kingdom family by Your Spirit and through my union with Your Son Jesus. I accept the wedding invitation. I ask that You would open my eyes that I may see the things You are revealing to me in the Bridal revelation.

Open my ears to hear Your voice clearer than ever before. Quicken my heart to know when Jesus steps into the room. Activate all of my spiritual senses and the ways that You desire to speak to me, in Jesus' name. I declare that I am the Bride of Christ.

Question to Ask Father God:

Father God, what did it cost You to find me, the Bride, for Your Son?

_____

_____

_____

_____

_____

Chapter Two

THE VALUE OF THE BRIDE

*D*id you know that you are so valuable that you are worth dying for? Jesus loves you so much that He gave up His life for you. He died for His Bride. He paid for a marriage relationship with His life. And His last words on the cross were to you:

"When he had sipped the sour wine, he said, 'It is finished, my bride!' Then he bowed his head and surrendered his spirit to God." (John 19:30 TPT)

Think about that... the last words of Jesus before giving up His life were to His Bride! The Hebrew word for "finished" used in this Scripture is "kalah" which means "fulfilled [completed]" and "bride" (see the passion translation commentary). These last words of Christ are of utmost importance.

Love Bears All Things

What does true love look like?

"Love is large and incredibly patient. Love is gentle and consistently kind to all. It refuses to be jealous when blessing comes to someone else. Love does not brag about one's achievements nor inflate its own importance. Love does not traffic in shame and disrespect, nor selfishly seek its own honor. Love is not easily irritated or quick to take offense. Love joyfully celebrates honesty and finds no delight in what is wrong. Love is a safe place of shelter, for it never stops believing the best for others. Love never takes failure as defeat, for it never gives up. Love never stops loving." (1 Corinthians 13:4-8 TPT)

Interestingly, Jesus' betrayal was marked by a *fake* kiss from Judas, who walked closely with Him all along. False intimacy was the symbol that led to His greatest persecution and death. Jesus suffered not only betrayal but physical violence, punishment, verbal abuse, and mocking. His clothes were ripped off of Him leaving Him violated and shamed.

How could He possibly bear it all? He endured all of that because of the intensity of His love for us—true love that "never stops loving." We are the joy that was set before Him, enabling Him to endure the Cross.

"We look away from the natural realm and we fasten our gaze onto Jesus who birthed faith within us and who leads us forward into faith's perfection. His example is this: Because his heart was focused on the joy of knowing that you would be his, he endured the agony of the cross and conquered its humiliation, and now sits exalted at the right hand of the throne of God! So consider carefully how Jesus faced such intense opposition from sinners who opposed their own souls, so that you won't become worn down and cave in under life's pressures." (Hebrews 12:2-3 TPT)

True love gives up one's life for another.

"This is how we have discovered love's reality: Jesus sacrificed his life for us." (1 John 3:16 TPT)

"I am the Good Shepherd who lays down my life as a sacrifice for the sheep." (John 10:11 TPT)

Jesus' love for us runs more deeply than we could ever imagine. Still having trouble believing you are worthy of such love? Read on.

No Longer Separated

There used to be a veil of separation between us and God. The veil in the temple that separated the Holy of Holies from the people was thicker than anything we could ever get through. Religious systems and rules of the old covenant, perverted by man's religion, were impossible to live up to.

But Jesus loved us too much to let it stay that way. It was His death on the cross that removed the veil of separation, enabling us to live in true intimacy with Him forever. Jesus paid the price for us to have direct access, to be able to run in boldly before the throne of grace (Hebrews 4:16).

"It is you I long for, with no veil between us!" (Song of Songs 1:7 TPT)

"Jesus passionately cried out, took his last breath, and gave up his spirit. At that moment the veil in the Holy of Holies was torn in two from the top to the bottom. The earth shook violently, rocks were split apart." (Matthew 27:50-51 TPT)

"For he has dedicated a new, life-giving way for us to approach God. For just as the veil was torn in two, Jesus' body was torn open to give us free and fresh access to him!" (Hebrews 10:20 TPT)

That act proves that we are worth dying for.

Our Worth as His Bride

It's hard to believe, isn't it, that we are so valuable to Him. Is it really true? Does He love us that much? I searched the Bible to find out, and I landed in Proverbs 31.

For almost all of my Christian walk with God, I've thought the "virtuous woman" in Proverbs 31 referred to how women are supposed to act and live. Although that perspective is true in part, there is a deeper meaning.

I've come to realize that the author of Song of Songs (one of my favorite books of the Bible) is the same one who authored Proverbs 31. Song of Songs and Proverbs 31 both contain a love letter between Jesus, the Bridegroom King Lover, and His Bride.

In the Scripture below, I want you to read with the reality of Jesus speaking to His Bride. This is what He thinks about all of us, men and women, as His Bride in relation to Himself as the Husband. Our worth is far above rubies.

"Who could ever find a wife like this one—she is a woman of strength and mighty valor! She's full of wealth and wisdom. The price paid for her was greater than many jewels. Her husband has entrusted his heart to her, for she brings him the rich spoils of victory. All throughout her life she brings him what is good and not evil. She searches out continually to possess that which is pure and righteous. She delights in the work of her hands. She gives out revelation-truth to feed others. She is like a trading ship bringing divine supplies from the merchant. Even in the night season she arises and sets food on the table for hungry ones in her house and for others. She sets her heart upon a nation and takes it as her own, carrying it within her. She labors there to plant the living vines.

She wraps herself in strength, might, and power in all her works. She tastes and experiences a better substance, and her shining light will not be extinguished, no matter how dark the night. She stretches out her hands to help the needy and she lays hold of the wheels of government. She is known by her extravagant generosity to the poor, for she always reaches out her hands to those in need. She is not afraid of tribulation, for all her household is covered in the dual garments of right-eousness and grace. Her clothing is beautifully knit together—a purple gown of exquisite linen. Her husband is famous and admired by all, sitting as the venerable judge of his people.

Even her works of righteousness she does for the benefit of her enemies.

Bold power and glorious majesty are wrapped around her as she laughs with joy over the latter days. Her teachings are filled with wisdom and kindness as loving instruction pours from her lips. She watches over the ways of her household and meets every need they have. Her sons and daughters arise in one accord to extol her virtues, and her husband arises to speak of her in glowing terms. "There are many valiant and noble ones, but you have ascended above them all!" Charm can be misleading, and beauty is vain and so quickly fades, but this virtuous woman lives in the wonder, awe, and fear of the Lord. She will be praised throughout eternity. So go ahead and give her the credit that is due, for she has become a radiant woman, and all her loving works of righteousness deserve to be admired at the gateways of every city!" (Proverbs 31:10-31 TPT)

Personal Encounter:

I had an encounter one time during worship where the Lord said to me, "Do you know what I had to go through just to be able to kiss you?" I had the sensation of Jesus, my Bridegroom King, kissing my cheek, just as the Shulamite Bride says, "Let Him smother me with kisses—his Spirit-Kiss divine" in Song of Songs 1:2 (TPT).

Immediately, I saw split second visions of Jesus being betrayed, beaten, persecuted, and then hanging on the cross. So much blood. I was broken in worship from the gravity of the price He paid to be intimately close to me.

Each time the Lord came closer, I became completely undone—weeping, worshiping, and receiving His love. Never could I feel unworthy again as He awakened me to His affection and thoughts toward me.

"Then they spat on his face and blindfolded him. Others struck him over and over with their fists and taunted him by saying, 'Prophesy to us! Tell us which one of us is about to hit you next?' and the guards took him and beat him." (Mark 14:65 TPT)

Activation Prayer:

Jesus, thank You for the price that You paid for me. I desire to live from the reality of my true worth. Break off every lie and every devaluing word that has ever been spoken to me or about me. I repent for every devaluing word that I've ever spoken over myself or others. Help me to love myself as You love me. Amen.

Questions to Ask Jesus:

Jesus, how do You feel about me? What do You want to show me about my value?

_____

_____

_____

_____

_____

Chapter Three

THE BRIDEGROOM'S PURSUIT OF YOU

"*N*ever again will you be called 'The Forsaken City' or 'The Desolate Land.' Your new name will be 'The City of God's Delight' and 'The Bride of God,' for the Lord delights in you and will claim you as his bride." (Isaiah 62:4 NLT

Jesus is claiming you as His Bride. He is pursuing you, knocking at the door of your heart, longing for deeper communion and closeness with you. Will you let Him in?

A Deeper Invitation

When people hear, "Jesus is knocking at the door of your heart," they often hear it as an invitation to accept salvation—if they open the door, they will be saved and will gain access to heaven one day when they die.

But there's a deeper invitation here. Opening the door to our heart opens realms of heaven to us *right now*. In other words, we get to experience and delight in Jesus' Kingdom here on earth.

One day in prayer, I was studying Revelation 3:20, and as I continued reading through to chapter 4, the Lord told me that when we open the door to our heart and let Him in, we are then seated with Him in heavenly realms and the "Throne Room" of heaven is accessible to us.

"Behold, I'm standing at the door, knocking. If your heart is open to hear my voice and you open the door within, I will come in to you and feast with you, and you will feast with me. And to the one who conquers I will give the privilege of sitting with me on my throne, just as I conquered and sat down with my Father on his throne. The one whose heart is open let him listen carefully to what the Spirit is saying now to the churches." (Revelation 3:20-22 TPT)

Did you hear that? "I will come in and feast with you." "I will give the privilege of sitting with me on my throne." Amazing!

What does His throne look like? What will we see there?

"Then suddenly, after I wrote down these messages, I saw a heavenly portal open before me, and the same trumpet-voice I heard speaking with me at the beginning broke the silence and said, 'Ascend into this realm! I want to reveal to you what must happen after this.' Instantly I was taken into the spirit realm, and behold—I saw a heavenly throne set in place and someone seated upon it. His appearance was sparkling like crystal and glowing like a carnelian gemstone.

Surrounding the throne was a circle of green light, like an emerald rainbow. Encircling the great throne were twenty-four thrones with elders in glistening white garments seated upon them, each wearing a golden crown of victory. And pulsing from the throne were blinding flashes of lightning, crashes of thunder, and voices. And burning before the throne are seven blazing torches, which represent the seven Spirits of God. And in front of the throne there was pavement like a crystal sea of glass.

Around the throne and on each side stood four living creatures, full of eyes in front and behind. The first living creature resembled a lion, the second an ox, the third had a human face, and the fourth was like an eagle in flight. Each of the four living creatures had six wings, full of eyes all around and under their wings. They worshiped without ceasing, day and night, singing, 'Holy, holy, holy is the Lord God, the Almighty! The Was, the Is, and the Coming!'" (Revelation 4:1-8 TPT)

What an incredible invitation this is, not only to be loved by this great King and Bridegroom, but to sit with Him on His throne. We must respond to the knocking to experience the heavenly realms here on earth. Is your heart open to His voice, to His love? Open the door and let Him in!

Hear Jesus Knocking

Jesus is radically in love with us. When He knocks at the door of our hearts, He is pursuing us, inviting us to come closer. Yet in the busyness of our lives, we can easily ignore His wooing. We don't always hear His knocking.

In moments where we feel His Presence or we notice something in creation that echoes His voice, we should pause and lean into Him. Those moments are opportunities to encounter Heavenly Bliss. Bridal encounters with Jesus happen when we can find stillness to be with Him.

Arise, My Love

Another place in the Bible where Jesus is knocking on the door for intimacy is in Song of Songs chapter 5. Read through this passage slowly. Listen for His invitation to you.

"After this I let my devotion slumber, but my heart for him stayed awake. I had a dream. I dreamed of my beloved—he was coming to me in the darkness of night. The melody of the man I love awakened me. I heard his knock at my heart's door as he pleaded with me: Arise, my love. Open your heart, my darling, deeper still to me. Will you receive me this dark night? There is no one else but you, my friend, my equal. I need you this night to arise and come be with me. You are my pure, loyal dove, a perfect partner for me. My flawless one, will you arise?

For my heaviness and tears are more than I can bear. I have spent myself for you throughout the dark night. I have already laid aside my own garments for you. How could I take them up again since I've yielded my righteousness to yours? You have cleansed my life and taken me so far. Isn't that enough? My beloved reached into me to unlock my heart. The core of my very being trembled at his touch. How my soul melted when he spoke to me! My spirit arose to open for more of his touch.

As I surrendered to him, I began to sense his fragrance—the fragrance of his suffering love! It was the sense of myrrh flowing all through me! I opened my soul to my beloved, but suddenly he was gone! And my heart was torn out in longing for him. I sought his presence, his fragrance, but could not find him anywhere. I called out for him, yet he did not answer me. I will arise and search for him until I find him." (Song of Songs 5:2-6 TPT)

Cast Out the Foxes

Song of Songs speaks much about our love relationship with the Lord. Jesus loves us so much that He wants absolutely nothing to get in the way of our relationship with Him—no other lovers, no lies, no distractions.

"You must catch the troubling foxes, those sly little foxes that hinder our relationship. For they raid our budding vineyard of love to ruin what I've planted within you. Will you catch them and remove them for me? We will do it together." (Song of Songs 2:15 TPT)

Jesus calls us to identify these "troubling foxes" that destroy the vines of intimacy and remove them from our love garden. In fact, He says, "We will do it together."

Are there any areas of your life that you feel like hinder your ability to be close with the Lord? What are the "little foxes" that destroy the vine of intimacy for you? Are there any lies that you are believing about yourself or about the Lord? If you aren't sure what these foxes might be, ask Him. He will tell you and help you get rid of them.

Awakening Desire

Jesus is looking for total surrender into His arms. As you say "Yes" to His pursuit of you, He awakens you at the core of your being with deeper intimacy than you ever knew was possible. He lavishes His affection on you in ways you never knew you needed.

I've read this next Scripture over and over again. I can't even count how many times. I went through a season of divine awakening to more Bridal Encounters with Him. I challenge you to read this Scripture with expectation of Jesus coming to awaken you.

"Who is this one? Look at her now! She arises out of her desert, clinging to her beloved. When I awakened you under the apple tree, as you were feasting upon me, I awakened your innermost being with the travail of birth as you longed for more of me. Fasten me upon your heart as a seal of fire forevermore. This living, consuming flame will seal you as my prisoner of love.

My passion is stronger than the chains of death and the grave, all-consuming as the very flashes of fire from the burning heart of God. Place this fierce, unrelenting fire over your entire being. Rivers of pain and persecution will never extinguish this flame. Endless floods will be unable to quench this raging fire that burns within you. Everything will be consumed. It will stop at nothing as you yield everything to this furious fire until it won't even seem to you like a sacrifice anymore." (Song of Songs 8:5-7 TPT)

Nothing can quench His fierce and passionate love for you. How will you respond to His invitation?

Personal Encounter:

I've had encounters of hearing audible knocking during the day and in the night while sleeping. In those moments, I know to go to Jesus and spend time with Him. He wants to be with me and feast with me.

When this first started happening, I would go to the door thinking someone was actually there. You may have similar experiences. Really, the point is that when you sense His presence in the middle of the day or awakening you out of your sleep at night, respond. However He is choosing to get your attention, respond.

Activation Prayer:

Lord, I open the door to my heart and welcome You in. Help me to become more aware of Your affections for me. Help me to sense, see, and hear Your love for me everyday and everywhere I go. Teach me how to yield to Your presence and to respond to Your pursuit of me. Amen.

Question to Ask Jesus:

Jesus, are there any areas of my life that I haven't let You into?

_____

_____

_____

_____

_____

Chapter Four

MARRIAGE COVENANT

When people get married, they enter into a covenant with each other, making unbreakable promises to one another.

Jesus does the same for us. Our marriage covenant with Him is known as the new covenant in the Bible. While the old covenant pointed to our desperate need for a Savior, the new covenant is His stunning declaration of love and commitment to us, an expression that He has already fulfilled our need for a Savior and brought us close to Him.

I, for one, am so thankful for the new covenant. I would have never made it under the old covenant conditions. With my life story, I would have been stoned a long time ago. (See the last section of this book for my whole story). But I think that sometimes we take the covenant we have with the Lord for granted. Let's take a glimpse at what we have.

Written on Our Hearts

Part of this covenant is that we will know the Lord so deeply that His Words will be written on our hearts. We will know His love intimately, and we will be one with Him.

"'The day is coming,' says the Lord, 'when I will make a new covenant with the people of Israel and Judah. This covenant will not be like the one I made with their ancestors when I took them by the hand and brought them out of the land of Egypt. They broke that covenant, though I loved them as a husband loves his wife,' says the Lord. 'But this is the new covenant I will make with the people of Israel after those days,' says the Lord. 'I will put my instructions deep within them, and I will write them on their hearts. I will be their God, and they will be my people. And they will not need to teach their neighbors, nor will they need to teach their relatives, saying, "You should know the Lord." For everyone, from the least to the greatest, will know me already,' says the Lord. 'And I will forgive their wickedness, and I will never again remember their sins.'" (Jeremiah 31:31-34 NLT)

Loyal Forever

In the old covenant, what seemed to upset God the most was when His people turned away from Him and would worship other gods or idols in their lives. God called them an adulterous generation.

He wants to be our First Love forever. While our hearts are still prone to wander and waiver, Jesus stands loyal, faithful in His love to us.

"The priests on earth serve in a temple that is but a copy modeled after the heavenly sanctuary; a shadow of the reality. For when Moses began to construct the tabernacle God warned him and said, 'You must precisely follow the pattern I revealed to you on Mount Sinai.' But now Jesus the Messiah has accepted a priestly ministry which far surpasses theirs, since he is the catalyst of a better covenant which contains far more wonderful promises! For if that first covenant had been faultless no one would have needed a second one to replace it. But God revealed the defect and limitation of the first when he said to his people, 'Look! The day will come, declares the Lord, when I will satisfy the people of Israel and Judah by giving them a new covenant.

It will be an entirely different covenant than the one I made with their fathers when I led them by my hand out of Egypt. For they did not remain faithful to my covenant, so I rejected them, says the Lord God. For here is the covenant I will one day establish with the people of Israel: I will embed my laws within their thoughts and fasten them onto their hearts. I will be their loyal God and they will be my loyal people. And the result of this will be that everyone will know me as Lord! There will be no need at all to teach their fellow-citizens or brothers by saying, "You should know the Lord Jehovah," since everyone will know me inwardly, from the most unlikely to the most distinguished. For I will demonstrate my mercy to them and will forgive their evil deeds, and never remember again their sins.' This proves that by establishing this new covenant the first is now obsolete, ready to expire, and about to disappear." (Hebrews 8:5-13 TPT)

Free From Guilt

Both of the passages above speak to the idea that God will forgive our evil deeds and never remember our sins again. We are forgiven and free.

Remember, the new covenant is only possible because Jesus fulfilled our need for a Savior. We are no longer separated from God, but drawn close. Our consciences have been cleansed. We have been made pure. We are free from guilt. And thus, we are free to enter the marriage covenant with everything that we have.

"Under the old covenant the blood of bulls, goats, and the ashes of a heifer were sprinkled on those who were defiled and effectively cleansed them outwardly from their ceremonial impurities. Yet how much more will the sacred blood of the Messiah thoroughly cleanse our consciences! For by the power of the eternal Spirit he has offered himself to God as the perfect Sacrifice that now frees us from our dead works to worship and serve the living God. So Jesus is the One who has enacted a new covenant with a new relationship with God so that those who accept the invitation will receive the eternal inheritance he has promised to his heirs. For he died to release us from the guilt of the violations committed under the first covenant." (Hebrews 9:13-15 TPT)

With Unveiled Faces

In the new covenant we have with Jesus, the veil of the old is removed. We can imagine this veil like a bridal veil, removed once the groom and bride are announced husband and wife. We get to see Him face to face. We get to experience more glory than what we read about in the old covenant.

May the Lord remove every veil over our eyes and kiss us with the new covenant.

"Yet how much more radiant is this new and glorious ministry of the Spirit that shines from us! For if the former ministry of condemnation was ushered in with a measure of glory, how much more does the ministry that imparts right-eousness far excel in glory. What once was glorious no longer holds any glory because of the increasingly greater glory that has replaced it. The fading ministry came with a portion of glory, but now we embrace the unfading ministry of a perma-nent impartation of glory. So then, with this amazing hope living in us, we step out in freedom and boldness to speak the truth.

We are not like Moses, who used a veil to hide the glory to

keep the Israelites from staring at him as it faded away. Their minds were closed and hardened, for even to this day that same veil comes over their minds when they hear the words of the former covenant. The veil has not yet been lifted from them, for it is only eliminated when one is joined to the Messiah. So until now, whenever the Old Testament is being read, the same blinding comes over their hearts. But the moment one turns to the Lord with an open heart, the veil is lifted and they see.

Now, the 'Lord' I'm referring to is the Holy Spirit, and wherever he is Lord, there is freedom. We can all draw close to him with the veil removed from our faces. And with no veil we all become like mirrors who brightly reflect the glory of the Lord Jesus. We are being transfigured into his very image as we move from one brighter level of glory to another. And this glorious transfiguration comes from the Lord, who is the Spirit." (2 Corinthians 3:8-18 TPT)

Divine Union with Christ

Taking communion is a powerful part of the New Covenant — we experience divine union with Jesus.

The bread of communion is His body broken for us. Jesus took our sickness, sins, and shame in His own body to the cross. He suffered our consequences and the punishment we deserved. We don't have to live punishing ourselves or accepting the accusations of our accuser, the enemy, any longer.

The wine of communion is His blood shed for us. His blood that poured from His precious body is what washes us whiter than snow. In taking communion, we apply the power of His blood over our lives just as the children of Israel applied the blood of the lamb over the doorposts of their homes (Exodus 12:7) and the spirit of death had to pass over their families.

As we spend time and communion with Jesus, as we feast with Him, we are reminded in our faith of the power of what He did for us and we realign our authority, even to the extent of healing miracles that can take place during this time. Communion is also a beautiful time of worship with invitation for divine encounter with Him. He gives us fresh bread, manna from heaven.

"Then he lifted up a loaf, and after praying a prayer of thanksgiving to God, he gave each of his apostles a piece of bread, saying, 'This loaf is my body, which is now being offered to you. Always eat it to remember me.' After supper was over, he lifted the cup again and said, 'This cup is my blood of the new covenant I make with you, and it will be poured out soon for all of you. But I want you to know that the hands of the one who delivers me to be the sacrifice are with mine on the table this very moment. The Son of Man must now go where he will be sacrificed. But there will be great and unending doom for the man who betrays me.' The apostles questioned among themselves which one of them was about to do this." (Luke 22:19-23 TPT)

Personal Encounter:

One evening in service, I saw Jesus riding into our sanctuary on the white horse as described in Revelation chapter 19. He was coming in His majesty. And He reached His hand out and lifted me onto His horse with Him. I leaned my face into His back and embraced Him around His waist. I was blended into the mantle of His robe as he galloped through galaxies.

We arrived in the new Jerusalem through a pearl gate. And Jesus went down the gold streets of heaven with me on His horse. The Lord said to me that He wants everyone to see His affection for me, and that I will never have to beg for His affection. He wants the world to know of His affection for me. He wants all of creation to witness His affection for me. So many kisses from Jesus. I felt the warmth of His love for me. I felt safe on His horse with Him, feeling the heat of His mantle around me as I was blended into Him.

In this vision, I represented His Bride. This is how Jesus feels about you! He wants all of heaven and earth to know that you have His affection, that He is in covenant with you!

Activation Prayer:

Jesus, I repent for every ungodly covenant that I have ever made. I repent for every time that I have violated my covenant with You. I enter fully into marriage covenant, the new covenant You paid for me to have. Amen.

Question to Ask Jesus:

What do You want to show me about the blessings and inheritance of the new covenant?

_____

_____

_____

_____

_____

Chapter Five

CARRYING THE NAME OF OUR HUSBAND

*J*esus has given us the authority of His name just as a wife carries the authority of her husband's last name. We are one with Jesus, and as His Bride, we can use His authority as we are led by Him. Just like I, as a wife, can legally sign my husband's name on some documents, I can sign Jesus' name and speak on His behalf. What power! What privilege! And what responsibility!

In my opinion, the Bride of Christ is the highest place of authority that an individual can walk in. We are seated in heavenly places with Him, above principalities and spiritual wickedness, sharing His throne and given the right to operate in His authority and power. Jesus gave us His keys of authority to reign in His kingdom with Him. The name of Jesus gives us authority over every unclean spirit and all sickness and disease (Matthew 10:1, Mark 3:14-15, Mark 6:7, Luke 9:1).

"Then Jesus came close to them and said, 'All the authority of the universe has been given to me. Now wherever you go, make disciples of all nations, baptizing them in the name of the Father, the Son, and the Holy Spirit. And teach them to faithfully follow all that I have commanded you. And never forget that I am with you every day, even to the completion of this age.'" (Matthew 28:18-20 TPT)

We don't use His name on our own. He is with us—*always*.

And He is counting on us to act on His behalf and for His glory.

The Power of His Name

The Bride carries the authority of the name Jesus:

1. Jesus is the highest name in all existence. (Philippians 2:9-11)
2. Whatever we ask in His name will be given to us. (John 14:13)
3. Anyone who calls on His name will be saved. (Romans 10:13)
4. Healing miracles, signs, and wonders are performed through His name. (Acts 4:30)
5. We are washed, sanctified, and justified in His name. (1 Corinthians 6:11)
6. We cast out demons in His name. (Mark 16:17)
7. His name is a strong tower that provides safety. (Proverbs 18:10)

We can see some examples of this in Scripture. When Peter and John passed by a crippled man begging, Peter declared, "I don't have money, but I'll give you this—by the power of the name of Jesus Christ of Nazareth, stand up and walk!" (Acts 3:6 TPT). And, indeed, the man jumped up, momentarily stunned, and then walked with the disciples into the Temple, praising God and giving Him glory.

And when the religious leaders were frightened by the miracles they saw the disciples doing and heard what they were teaching the crowds, they actually tried to forbid the disciples from speaking Jesus' name (see Acts 4-5). They knew the power that it had!

Using the Name of Jesus

But it's not just in the Scriptures. Jesus' name holds power today, too! When we use the name of our Husband Jesus, it must be in accordance with His will, His Word, and His character. That is why it is so vital to be in a loving relationship with Him—so that we know His heart and desires, and can speak on His behalf!

Misusing His Name

Jesus' name is powerful. There is no doubt about that. Yet there are some who *abuse* the name of Jesus. They use His name and His authority, while having absolutely no relationship with Jesus. It never turns out good for them.

"Now, there were seven itinerant Jewish exorcists, sons of Sceva the high priest, who took it upon themselves to use the name and authority of Jesus over those who were demonized. They would say, 'We cast you out in the name of the Jesus that Paul preaches!' One day, when they said those words, the demon in the man replied, 'I know about Jesus, and I recognize Paul, but who do you think you are?' Then the demonized man jumped on them and threw them to the ground, beating them mercilessly. He overpowered the seven exorcists until they all ran out of the house naked and badly bruised. All of the people in Ephesus were awestruck, both Jews and non-Jews, when they heard about what had happened. Great fear fell over the entire city, and the authority of the name of Jesus was exalted. Many believers publicly confessed their sins and disclosed their secrets. Large numbers of those who had been practicing magic took all of their books and scrolls of spells and incantations and publicly burned them. When the value of all the books and scrolls was calculated, it all came to several million dollars. The power of God caused the word to spread, and the people were greatly impacted." (Acts 19:13-20 TPT)

Another place in Scripture where we see people using the name of Jesus without relationship is in Matthew chapter seven. "Not everyone who says to me, 'Lord, Lord,' will enter into the realm of heaven's kingdom. It is only those who persist in doing the will of my heavenly Father. On the day of judgment many will say to me, 'Lord, Lord, don't you remember us? Didn't we prophesy in your name? Didn't we cast out demons and do many miracles for the sake of your name?' But I will have to say to them, 'Go away from me, you lawless rebels! I've never been joined to you!'" (Matthew 7:21-23 TPT)

We have to take a look at our motives in ministry. The purest form of ministry flows from love and total devotion to Jesus.

Making His Name Glorious

When you speak the name of Jesus, what is going on in your heart? Are you doing it out of a relationship with Him, your Bridegroom? Are you speaking on behalf of your Husband? Or are you doing it to draw attention to yourself or for selfish reasons? When we use Jesus' name, we give others a glimpse of His glory and power. Let's not be like those who misuse His name for their own purposes. Let's cry out with the psalmist, "Join me, everyone! Let's praise the Lord together. Let's make him famous! Let's make his name glorious to all" (Psalm 34:3 TPT).

Personal Encounter:

During a time of prayer, I heard the Lord say to me, "You are my beloved Bride. To, whom I give the authority to use my name... To act on My behalf in the earth. My name marks you in the Spirit. You are Mine and I am yours. You have been given the right to carry the fullness of My name, my Bride."

Then I was taken into a vision, where I saw myself holding His name in my hands. I would release His name and His name would accomplish Kingdom exploits and manifestations of His Word. The action of using His name in faith was almost like a currency of sorts, with the highest legal authority to align things with the Will of God.

"They will see constantly His face, and His name will be on their foreheads." (Revelation 22:4 TPT)

Activation Prayer:

Jesus, I receive Your name in my marriage covenant with You. I acknowledge the power and authority I have through Your name. I ask that You raise my faith and reveal to me everything I have because of Your name. Forgive me if I have ever abused the use of Your name. Your name is holy and above all names. Hallelujah! Amen.

Question to Ask Jesus:

Jesus, can You show me the areas of my life that I need to apply the power of Your name?

_____

_____

_____

_____

_____

Chapter Six

A BRIDE WITHOUT SPOT OR BLEMISH

We are being prepared for our Bridegroom, Jesus. And part of that preparation is being made clean and whole, new and fresh. Fortunately, this is not work that we have to do ourselves. Through Christ, we are redeemed and made new.

"Then in a vision I saw a new heaven and a new earth. The first heaven and earth had passed away, and the sea no longer existed. I saw the Holy City, the New Jerusalem, descending out of the heavenly realm from the presence of God, like a pleasing bride that had been prepared for her husband, adorned for her wedding. And I heard a thunderous voice from the throne, saying: 'Look! God's tabernacle is with human beings. And from now on he will tabernacle with them as their God.

Now God himself will have his home with them—"God-with-them" will be their God! He will wipe away every tear from their eyes and eliminate death entirely. No one will mourn or weep any longer. The pain of wounds will no longer exist, for the old order has ceased.' And God-Enthroned spoke to me and said, 'Consider this! I am making everything to be new and fresh. Write down at once all that I have told you, because each word is trustworthy and dependable.'" (Revelation 21:1-5 TPT)

"We look away from the natural realm and we fasten our gaze onto Jesus who birthed faith within us and who leads us forward into faith's perfection." (Hebrews 12:2 TPT)

What does this look like? In what ways will we be made new? How will our faith be perfected? The Lord desires to redeem every part of our lives. Healing is possible. Purity is possible through Christ. Freedom is possible.

Healing

One day, we will have absolutely no more death, tears, sickness, or pain. Yet experiencing glimpses of heaven is possible even now. Healing and deliverance are available to us as the Bride.

"But he was pierced for our rebellion, crushed for our sins. He was beaten so we could be whole. He was whipped so we could be healed." (Isaiah 53:5 NLT)

"He personally carried our sins in his body on the cross so that we can be dead to sin and live for what is right. By his wounds you are healed." (1 Peter 2:24 NLT)

Not only did Christ die for our sins, but He purchased our healing as well. *"By his wounds you are healed."* It is because of the price He paid that we have a right to be healed physically and emotionally. And as His Bride, we have the privilege of releasing healing to others as we advance His Kingdom.

Freedom from Sin and Oppression

He is jealous over us. We must rid ourselves of every other lover, every continual sin, and every other idol. Freedom comes from complete surrender through encounter with Jesus. It's not necessarily something that we have to strive or labor for. It's more about loving and knowing the One who is truth, and the truth sets us free. He washes over us with His truths as we humble ourselves before Him.

"If you embrace the truth, it will release more freedom into your lives." (John 8:32 TPT)

"So if the Son sets you free from sin, then become a true son and be unquestioningly free!" (John 8:36 TPT)

If you focus on your mistakes and sins from a perspective of trying to attain perfection, you will never succeed. If you focus on being so in love with Jesus that you want to please Him, then before you know it, sins and habits of the past pale in comparison to Him.

Going back to old sin feels like a dog returning to vomit (Proverbs 26:11) because you've experienced a higher reality of bliss: the loveliness of Jesus. Jesus is the only one that can fulfill voids and longings of the soul. We were always meant to be married to Him.

"Let me be clear, the Anointed One has set us free—not partially, but completely and wonderfully free! We must always cherish this truth and stubbornly refuse to go back into the bondage of our past." (Galatians 5:1 TPT)

Holy and Clean

There is a great mystery revealed about Jesus as our Husband and us as His wife. See if you can capture it.

"And further, submit to one another out of reverence for Christ. For wives, this means submit to your husbands as to the Lord. For a husband is the head of his wife as Christ is the head of the church. He is the Savior of his body, the church. As the church submits to Christ, so you wives should submit to your husbands in everything. For husbands, this means love your wives, just as Christ loved the church. He gave up his life for her to make her holy and clean, washed by the cleansing of God's word.

He did this to present her to himself as a glorious church without a spot or wrinkle or any other blemish. Instead, she will be holy and without fault. In the same way, husbands ought to love their wives as they love their own bodies. For a man who loves his wife actually shows love for himself. No one hates his own body but feeds and cares for it, just as Christ cares for the church. And we are members of his body. As the Scriptures say, 'A man leaves his father and mother and is joined to his wife, and the two are united into one.' This is a great mystery, but it is an illustration of the way Christ and the church are one. So again I say, each man must love his wife as he loves himself, and the wife must respect her husband." (Ephesians 5:21-33 NLT)

Jesus washes over us to present us as glorious without spot or wrinkle or any blemish. This is only possible through His death for us as the Passover Lamb of God.

All of this discussion about husbands and wives is very applicable in the natural, but I also love the deeper meaning. Another translation says it like this: "This is a great mystery, but I speak concerning Christ and the church" (Ephesians 5:32 NKJV). Look at His overwhelming love for us!

"You need to know that God's passion is burning inside me for you, because, like a loving father, I have pledged your hand in marriage to Christ, your true bridegroom. I've also promised that I would present his fiancée to him as a pure virgin bride." (2 Corinthians 11:2 TPT)

"And so, dear brothers and sisters, I plead with you to give your bodies to God because of all he has done for you. Let them be a living and holy sacrifice—the kind he will find acceptable. This is truly the way to worship him. Don't copy the behavior and customs of this world, but let God transform you into a new person by changing the way you think. Then you will learn to know God's will for you, which is good and pleasing and perfect." (Romans 12:1-2 NLT)

Trust Him

As you are allowing Jesus to wash over you and purify you through His Word and the fire of His Spirit, I have a question to ask you: Do you fully trust Jesus with your heart?

It is challenging to be intimate or close with someone that you don't fully trust. If you have had lovers, friends, parents, spiritual leaders, or anyone in a "primary relationship" wound you or betray you, sometimes we subconsciously assume that Jesus is going to treat us the same way.

If this seems to be resonating with you, then ask Jesus if there is anyone that you need to forgive and release. Break any lie that Jesus is like the person or people who hurt you. It is possible to love someone, but not trust them. In order to experience the fullness of His love, you have to love and trust Jesus with your whole heart.

If there are any areas of your life where you are finding it challenging to trust Jesus, surrender those areas to Him. Ask Jesus to show you what trusting Him really looks like.

Radiant Beauty

"Every part of you is so beautiful, my darling. Perfect is your beauty, without flaw within. Now you are ready, my bride, to come with me as we climb the highest peaks together. Come with me through the archway of trust. We will look down from the crest of the glistening mounts and from the summit of our sublime sanctuary. Together we will wage war in the lion's den and the leopard's lair as they watch nightly for their prey." (Song of Songs 4:7-8 TPT)

I can't even count the number of encounters that I've had with Jesus washing over me, healing me, delivering me. With all that I've been through in life, I have learned to stay humble and teachable to the Lord. He is so faithful.

There are always areas that we can learn, grow, and become more like Him. If there is a "spot" in your life that Jesus seems to be pointing to, it is never to condemn you or make you feel shame, but it's because He loves you so much that He wants to wash over you and set you free.

Spend time with Jesus. Talk to Him about the pressing issues in your life. Ask Him questions and wait for Him to speak to you. Don't make assumptions with head knowledge, but respond to the things that He reveals to you with humility, repentance, forgiveness, or whatever action He leads you to do.

"The Son is the dazzling radiance of God's splendor, the exact expression of God's true nature—his mirror image! He holds the universe together and expands it by the mighty power of his spoken word. He accomplished for us the complete cleansing of sins, and then took his seat on the highest throne at the right hand of the majestic One." (Hebrews 1:3 TPT)

Personal Encounter:

A couple of years ago, I was the speaker for a women's conference titled "Captivated." I was honored to be the main speaker of three sessions and the subject was chosen in advance by the women's ministry team who invited me.

It was the first time that I saw Jesus heal all (Matthew 8:16). I had been seeing the healing miracles of the Lord through personal evangelism and in the services of our church, Impact Life Church in Destin, FL. But this was the first time I heard Jesus say, "I am going to heal all." I think the focus of the conference had something to do with it. A group of about 400 women were so hungry to be captivated by Jesus. All of our focus was on our loving obsession with Him.

Some were sovereignly healed during the sermon time. Then, during altar prayer on the first night, I was led to stay late after the service was dismissed to pray for everyone who needed healing. I didn't finish until after 1am. Every woman present that had an ailment or sickness received healing miracles from Jesus! Hallelujah! I'm still so in awe of what the Lord did for the precious women who were captivated by Him.

I'm sharing this testimony to encourage you in your pursuit of Him. As you go deeper in love with the Lord, healing is a byproduct of His Kingship in our lives. If you have been suffering with a long-term medical condition, I am believing for your miracle in Jesus' name. Be encouraged and continue living captivated by Him.

Activation Prayer:

"Pray like this: Our Father in heaven, may your name be kept holy. May your Kingdom come soon. May your will be done on earth, as it is in heaven. Give us today the food we need, and forgive us our sins, as we have forgiven those who sin against us. And don't let us yield to temptation, but rescue us from the evil one.

"If you forgive those who sin against you, your heavenly Father will forgive you. But if you refuse to forgive others, your Father will not forgive your sins." (Matthew 6:9-15 NLT)

———

Questions to Ask Jesus:

Who do I need to forgive and release? Is there anything I need to forgive myself for? (Matthew 18:21-35)

_____

_____

_____

_____

_____

Chapter Seven

THE SWEET LOVELINESS OF HIS FACE

hen we are in seasons of pruning or correction (of being made pure and spotless), it can sometimes be challenging to see the light at the end of the tunnel. If you find yourself in one of those seasons now, be encouraged because the "light" at the end is the beautiful face of Jesus.

"I had only heard about you before, but now I have seen you with my own eyes." (Job 42:5 NLT)

"Lord, when you said to me, 'Seek my face,' my inner being responded, 'I'm seeking your face with all my heart.'" (Psalms 27:8 TPT)

We are to guard our hearts and keep ourselves pure. In doing so, Jesus Himself is our reward.

"What bliss you experience when your heart is pure! For then your eyes will be open to see more and more of God." (Matthew 5:8 TPT)

Face to Face with Jesus

Gazing into the face of Jesus causes the brilliant light of the glorious knowledge of God to cascade into us. Hallelujah! In Him, we can find everything that we need.

"We don't preach ourselves, but rather the lordship of Jesus Christ, for we are your servants for Jesus' sake. For God, who said, 'Let brilliant light shine out of darkness,' is the one who has cascaded his light into us—the brilliant dawning light of the glorious knowledge of God as we gaze into the face of Jesus Christ." (2 Corinthians 4:5-6 TPT)

Do you see His face as beautiful? Do you seek the pleasure of Him? As you read the following passage, see how many elements we have already talked about.

"Who, then, ascends into the presence of the Lord? And who has the privilege of entering into God's Holy Place? Those who are clean—whose works and ways are pure, whose hearts are true and sealed by the truth, those who never deceive, whose words are sure. They will receive the Lord's blessing and righteousness given by the Savior-God. They will stand before God, for they seek the pleasure of God's face, the God of Jacob. *Pause in his presence.*" (Psalm 24:3-6 TPT)

Go ahead, pause in His presence. Gaze upon His face. Stand before God in intimacy and love. He is glorious.

Transformed by Him

Our times of intimacy with the Lord completely transform us. Sometimes we don't even realize the fullness of what He is doing.

For example, as we spend time with Jesus, His Spirit grows His fruit within us: love, joy, peace, patience, kindness, goodness, faithfulness, gentleness, and self-control (Galatians 5:22-23). These characteristics describe our Bridegroom. He is love. He is joy. He is peace. And as we are in union with Him, we become more like Him.

Think about the people who spent intimate time with the Lord in the Bible and how lives were changed in every encounter with Him. Upon encountering Jesus on the way to Damascus, Saul left a life of persecuting the Church and began to preach the Good News instead. It was such a big change that he even went by a different name: Paul.

I especially remember Moses, who literally wore a veil over his face after he spoke face to face with God because his time with the Lord left his face shining radiantly.

"When Moses came down from Mount Sinai with the two tablets of the covenant law in his hands, he was not aware that his face was radiant because he had spoken with the Lord.... When Moses finished speaking to them, he put a veil over his face. But whenever he entered the Lord's presence to speak with him, he removed the veil until he came out. And when he came out and told the Israelites what he had been commanded, they saw that his face was radiant. Then Moses would put the veil back over his face until he went in to speak with the Lord. (Exodus 34:29, 33-35 NIV)

It is the same now: as we behold His lovely face and spend time with Him, we experience transformation. Yet, unlike Moses, we don't veil our faces.

"We are not like Moses, who used a veil to hide the glory to keep the Israelites from staring at him as it faded away... We can all draw close to him with the veil removed from our faces. And with no veil we all become like mirrors who brightly reflect the glory of the Lord Jesus. We are being transfigured into his very image as we move from one brighter level of glory to another. And this glorious transfiguration comes from the Lord, who is the Spirit." (2 Corinthians 3:13, 18 TPT)

We are transformed as we live in union with Him. But we must draw close. We must remove the veil, or let Him remove it for us. We must see Him face to face.

"...be transformed as you embrace the glorious Christ-within as your new life and live in union with him! For God has re-created you all over again in his perfect righteousness, and you now belong to him in the realm of true holiness." (Ephesians 4:24, TPT)

The Glory of His Presence

Seeing the face of our Bridegroom is a place of such intimacy. Such grace. Let a longing and a hunger rise inside of you to see the face of God, to be in His presence.

"Here's the one thing I crave from God, the one thing I seek above all else: I want the privilege of living with him every moment in his house, finding the sweet loveliness of his face, filled with awe, delighting in his glory and grace. I want to live my life so close to him that he takes pleasure in my every prayer. In his shelter in the day of trouble, that's where you'll find me, for he hides me there in his holiness. He has smuggled me into his secret place, where I'm kept safe and secure—out of reach from all my enemies. Triumphant now, I'll bring him my offerings of praise, singing and shouting with ecstatic joy! Yes, listen and you can hear the fanfare of my shouts of praise to the Lord!" (Psalm 27:4-6 TPT)

Yet, several times in the Old Testament, God would "hide His face" from His people when they were rebelling (Deuteronomy 32:20, Micah 3:4, Ezekiel 39:23). David said many times in the book of Psalms, "Don't hide your face from me" which carried the same weight as "don't take your Spirit from me." Can you hear the gravity in his voice? His desperation? Not being able to see God's face was a devastating blow.

Have you ever been in that place where you longed for more of God? Where you found it hard to sense His presence? Or perhaps you have "tasted" of His glorious presence and want more of Him. I pray this passage will become a cry of your heart:

"I long to drink of you, O God, drinking deeply from the

streams of pleasure flowing from your presence. My longings overwhelm me for more of you! My soul thirsts, pants, and longs for the living God. I want to come and see the face of God." (Psalm 42:1-2 TPT)

Seek His face. Gaze upon Him, and let your Bridegroom transform you. It's a beautiful, radiant encounter with your greatest Love.

Personal Encounter:

One day, I was working late trying to handle more on my "to do" list. I heard the Lord whisper to me, "You can keep working, or you can spend time with Me." I instantly felt His presence and saw a vision of a whirlwind in the ceiling of my office. It was as if the ceiling was disappearing.

I got up from my desk and took a seat on the floor leaning up against the wall. Everything in my office got supernaturally cloudy except for one thing: a picture of the face of Jesus painted by Akiane Kramarik at age 8. Everything else was completely blurry in the room and all I could see was His face. I took the hint that Jesus wanted me to focus on His face. As I was gazing at Him and envisioning His fiery eyes of passion, I heard Him say, "You don't know how special you are. Let Me show you."

Instantly, in a trance-like encounter, I was taken to a heavenly place. Jesus took me into an indescribable hallway. I don't have adequate words to explain, but I will try. There were pictures on a wall that seemed to have no end. I had an inner knowing that I was in the "Hall of Generals." He showed me my face in one of the frames and I was moving and wearing a beautiful crown. Jesus said they are "moving pictures." Anyone in heaven could walk up and lean in to see things that people of faith had accomplished for Jesus. There were frames of people from the past, present, and future. I was in shock as to why my face was represented there. I saw stadiums of people, rainbow colors, and then I was back in my office being shaken in the manifested Glory of God.

After I somewhat sobered up, Jesus told me to look up "Hall of Generals" with a specific minister's name. Lo and behold, this individual was explaining a heavenly encounter in the exact same heavenly place... with moving pictures of Generals and Intercessors. It was so important for Jesus to show me how He sees me, which all started from me adoring and worshiping Him while looking at His face.

Shortly after this wild and glorious encounter, two of my friends, Stephanie and Tara, showed up because we were going out for Strip Club Ministry together. We went into a time of prayer, and immediately, Stephanie saw a whirlwind and the face of Jesus! Tara had an encounter with rainbow colors. It was as if they immediately stepped into the experience I just had with Jesus, and I did not say a thing to them about it beforehand.

My point in sharing this is that beautiful encounters can happen as we focus on the sweet loveliness of His face. We must not belittle the importance of intercession, for God's value system in heaven is much different than ours on earth. As we gaze upon Him, He speaks to us and higher realms of revelations open up.

"I have set the Lord continually before me; because he is at my right hand, I will not be shaken." (Psalm 16:8 NASB)

Activation Prayer:

Jesus, open my spiritual eyes to be able to see glimpses of You. I desire to behold Your face and encounter You in this way. I ask that You give me the grace to wait in Your presence until You move, speak, or show me something. Help me to empty my mind of distractions and focus on You. Lord, make Your face shine on me and be gracious to me. Lift up Your countenance on me and give me peace. Amen.

"The LORD make His face shine on you, And be gracious to you; The LORD lift up His countenance on you, And give you peace." (Numbers 6:25-26 NASB)

Question to Ask Jesus:

Jesus, can You show me Your face?

_____

_____

_____

_____

_____

Chapter Eight

INTIMACY WITH JESUS

$\mathcal{W}$ hen we draw near to our Bridegroom, we get to share in such intimate encounters with Him. It is glorious and divine.

"And when I passed by again, I saw that you were old enough for love. So I wrapped my cloak around you to cover your nakedness and declared my marriage vows. I made a covenant with you, says the Sovereign Lord, and you became mine." (Ezekiel 16:8 NLT)

This is a poem that I wrote on March 3, 2018. I pray that it will speak to you.

"Eternally HIS" Poem by Sula Skiles

I feel HIS PRESENCE enter the room... HE is approaching... Every fiber of my being jumps, dances and screams to collide with HIM... To crash into HIM... To be fully submerged in HIM... My eyes survey the atmosphere longing to be fixed on my BRIDEGROOM LOVER... I've been waiting... Waiting with my BURNING lamp overflowing with oil... Knowing that at any second, HE could pass by.... Waiting and yearning to catch a glimpse of HIS SPLENDOR... To see a FLASH of HIS fiery eyes of PASSION for me... There are natural noises around me, movements & voices of others. Don't they realize the BRIDEGROOM KING is making an entrance? I can't afford to miss the fullness of HIM... I can't afford to be robbed of INTIMACY with my LOVER. I move and REPOSITION myself so that the distractions around me fade away... Ohhhhhhhhhh!!! HE is closer... The one that I love. I sense WAVES of GLORY approaching!!! HE is here! I see HIM! He came! With all that I am, every cell in my body, I WORSHIP and ADORE HIM! I pour out my life on HIM as a drink offering, a living sacrifice. HE sees me. HE knows me. I am one of the ones, the JOY set before HIM, HIS reason for enduring the CROSS... HE approaches me and surges of ELECTRIC LIGHTNINGS OF GLORY hit the core of my being... HE can't resist me. HE wraps HIMSELF around me. I'm INTOXICATED by HIM. I'm completely undone. I melt into HIM and we are ONE.

The Private Intimacy of the Secret Place

"There's a private place reserved for the lovers of God, where they sit near Him and receive the revelation-secrets of His promises." (Psalm 25:14 TPT)

Jesus is the most faithful lover. He alone fully satisfies the soul. There is a secret place of prayer, encounters, and close-ness with Jesus. In daily devotion to Him, He reveals mysteries, secrets, and things that are to come.

For many years, I felt like reading the Bible and praying daily was more of a chore than a delight. I think that people don't realize how adventurous conversations and experiences with the Lord can be.

"But continue to grow and increase in God's grace and inti-macy with our Lord and Savior, Jesus Christ. May he receive all the glory both now and until the day eternity begins. Amen!" (2 Peter 3:18 TPT)

Our intimacy with Jesus affects our households. I've had several beautiful experiences with my kids, Zetta and Zane. There are times where Jesus is speaking to me about a certain revelation in the secret place of prayer. Then my children will have dreams and visions about the same topic within 24 hours, without knowing what I was experiencing. There is a literal Open Heaven over our homes when we spend time with Jesus. The Lord speaks to children with so much ease, because they have never learned religious mindsets and their hearts are pure. I encourage you, in your pursuit of Jesus, to believe in faith that your intimacy with Him will tremendously affect your future generations.

One evening in particular, I was reading about the Prophetess and Judge Deborah. Her story had my attention because, on two separate occasions within a week, I met two Deborahs standing next to each other who didn't know each other. I got the bright idea to look into this in Scripture. That's how revelation comes to me sometimes. I will hear Jesus speak a Scripture to me in the secret place or in everyday life, and then it seems as though the Word is surrounding me everywhere.

One evening, after putting the kids to bed, I was reading the following Scripture and praying into what Jesus might be saying to me.

"Deborah, the wife of Lappidoth, was a prophet who was judging Israel at that time. She would sit under the Palm of Deborah, between Ramah and Bethel in the hill country of Ephraim, and the Israelites would go to her for judgment." (Judges 4:4-5 NLT)

The next morning, Zetta, at age 7, woke up and ran in, telling me that she had a dream. She said she was sitting on a beautiful little island under a palm tree. The Lord told her to build a boat out of palm trees to go to the place that He was sending her. Then out of the sky, four palm trees fell in addition to the one that she was sitting under. The trees started forming into a little boat just for her. She got onto her boat and started sailing. At one point, a huge fancy cruise ship pulled up next to her and instantly she was on it. It was luxurious and full of masses of people. Zetta thought to herself, "I know I can stay here if I want, but I can't afford to. Lord, please put me back on my little palm tree boat." And she finished sailing to the place that God was sending her. She was full of joy when she arrived on shore and the dream ended.

The Lord gave me a beautiful interpretation for this dream. In short, we must remain in the secret place with Him to fulfil the calling on our lives. That is the place of grace. We can't afford to be distracted by what everyone else is doing or follow the masses. Obedience to Him matters most. Arriving to the place He is sending us is what matters most. He will provide the very vehicle of ministry that He is anointing us to move in. Our joy comes from following His voice.

Zetta did not hear me reading the Scriptures the night before. I think that it is so incredible that God can speak a Word to anyone in the house. When my kids encounter Jesus, I listen and steward what they say. They know that their experiences, dreams, and visions are valued no matter how simple or profound.

"God conceals the revelation of his word in the hiding place of his glory. But the honor of kings is revealed by how they thoroughly search out the deeper meaning of all that God says. The heart of a king is full of understanding, like the heavens are high and the ocean is deep." (Proverbs 25:2-3 TPT)

As you study the Bible, know that there are encounters that you are invited into. The Scriptures are truths to experience and ascend into through Jesus. Be awakened to greater intimacy with Jesus in your daily times of prayer. Be awakened to His affections for you. Do you know how He feels about you?

The Bridegroom King says to us:

"For you reach into my heart. With one flash of your eyes I am undone by your love, my beloved, my equal, my bride. You leave me breathless—I am overcome by merely a glance from your worshiping eyes, for you have stolen my heart. I am held hostage by your love and by the graces of righteousness shining upon you. How satisfying to me, my equal, my bride. Your love is my finest wine—intoxicating and thrilling. And your sweet, perfumed praises—so exotic, so pleasing." (Song of Songs 4:9-10 TPT)

Public Displays of Affection (PDA)

When you are so intimate with Jesus in the secret place, sometimes He chooses to lavish His love on you in public, what I call Public Displays of Affection. In those moments, yield to Him and do not focus on what people may be thinking around you. Just focus on Him. Do not allow others to distract you from His face.

If the Glory of the Lord begins hitting you in waves of electricity, fire, or however He wants to move, just surrender. This may be in a corporate setting of worship at church, or it could be while you're taking a walk, shopping in the store, anywhere.

I am learning to yield to Him whenever He shows up. Don't worry about looking foolish; just worship. When Jesus comes into the room, it is hard to contain yourself. Sadly, everyone doesn't always recognize Him when He comes.

"Yes, and I am willing to look even more foolish than this, even to be humiliated in my own eyes." (2 Samuel 6:22 NLT)

"My heart has heard you say, 'Come and talk with me.' And my heart responds, 'Lord, I am coming.'" (Psalms 27:8 NLT)

Intimacy with Jesus

There are several ways that you can experience Jesus. Don't get stuck in one way of hearing. I pray that fresh ways of encountering Jesus would crack open in your life as you read the following Scriptures. These are just a few of the ways we can experience Him as the Bride. Allow the Word to impart supernatural experiences to you.

His Voice

We can hear the voice of the Lord in prayer as we wait on Him to speak. Sometimes we hear His voice in the reading of His Word, the Bible.

"For we have the living Word of God, which is full of energy, like a two-mouthed sword. It will even penetrate to the very core of our being where soul and spirit, bone and marrow meet! It interprets and reveals the true thoughts and secret motives of our hearts." (Hebrews 4:12 TPT)

"My own sheep will hear my voice and I will know each one, and they will follow me." (John 10:27 TPT)

Dreams

All over the Bible, we see accounts of God speaking to people in dreams. The symbolic language of God in dreams is fascinating.

"In a dream, in a vision of the night, When deep sleep falls upon men, While slumbering on their beds, Then He opens the ears of men, And seals their instruction." (Job 33:15-16 NKJV)

Visions

"When there is no clear prophetic vision, people quickly wander astray. But when you follow the revelation of the word, heaven's bliss fills your soul." (Proverbs 29:18 TPT)

Here are several accounts in the word of visions that brought messages and direction from God: Daniel 7:13-14, Numbers 12:6, Acts 9:10-12, Acts 16:9, Isaiah 6:1-13, and Genesis 15:1

Trances and Heavenly Encounters

In a trance, the whole world seems to disappear as you begin to see what is being revealed to you from heaven. The word "trance" may seem weird to you if you have never had an experience like this before, but there are trance encounters in Scripture to read and study. When heaven comes, you can't always wrap your natural brain around it.

Here is one example of how trances occur:

"The next day around noon, as Cornelius' men were approaching Joppa, Peter went up to the flat roof of the house to pray. He was hungry and wanted to eat, but while lunch was being prepared he fell into a trance and entered into another realm. As the heavenly realm opened up, he saw something resembling a large linen tablecloth that descended from above, being let down to the earth by its four corners. As it floated down he saw that it held many kinds of four-footed animals, reptiles, and wild birds.

"A voice said to him, 'Peter, go and prepare them to be eaten.'

Peter replied, 'There's no way I could do that, Lord, for I've never eaten anything forbidden or impure according to our Jewish laws.'

The voice spoke again. 'Nothing is unclean if God declares it to be clean.' The vision was repeated three times. Then suddenly the linen sheet was snatched back up into heaven.

Peter was so stunned by the vision that he couldn't stop wondering about what all it meant. Meanwhile, Cornelius' men had learned where Peter was staying and at that same moment were standing outside the gate. They called out to those in the house, 'Is this where Simon, the Rock, is staying?'

As Peter was in deep thought, trying to interpret the vision, the Spirit said to him, 'Go downstairs now, for three men are looking for you. Don't hesitate to go with them, because I have sent them.'

Peter went downstairs to the men and said, 'I believe I'm the one you're looking for. What brings you here?'

They answered, 'We serve Cornelius, a Roman military captain, who sent us to find you. He is a devout man of the highest integrity who worships God and is respected throughout the Jewish community. He was divinely instructed through the appearance of an angel to summon you to his home and to listen to the message that you would bring him.'" (Acts 10:9-22 TPT)

Here are more trances and heavenly encounters to read: Ezekiel 8:1-3, Acts 22:17, and Revelation 1:10.

Ascending with Him

"Although it may not accomplish a thing, I need to move on and boast about supernatural visions and revelations of the Lord. Someone I'm acquainted with, who is in union with Christ, was swept away fourteen years ago in an ecstatic experience. He was taken into the third heaven, but I'm not sure if he was in his body or out of his body—only God knows. And I know that this man (again, I'm not sure if he was still in his body or taken out of his body—God knows) was caught up in an ecstatic experience and brought into paradise, where he overheard many wondrous and inexpressible secrets that were so sacred that no mortal is permitted to repeat them." (2 Corinthians 12:1-4 TPT)

"He raised us up with Christ the exalted One, and we ascended with him into the glorious perfection and authority of the heavenly realm, for we are now co-seated as one with Christ!" (Ephesians 2:6 TPT)

Here are more ascension encounters in the Word to read: Ezekiel 3:12-13; Song of Songs 2:4, 4:8, 6:12, 8:4; and Revelation 4:2, 21:10, 17:3.

Signs and Wonders

Signs and wonders appear in many forms, whether it's feathers appearing out of thin air, gold or diamond dust, manna, gemstones... Basically, the reality of heaven is so strong that heavenly substances jump from the unseen realm into the natural. There is always a message in the sign or wonder.

Jesus is King of Glory and King of Angel Armies. When He shows up, heaven, angels, and glory come with Him. I've learned to steward the signs and wonders as they appear. Thank God for Ziploc bags. Ha ha! I literally keep a Ziploc in my purse. I live in expectation of heaven showing up. I don't seek the wonders; they just happen to follow me because I'm in love with my Husband, Jesus. I have a treasure chest at home where I keep every precious gift from heaven. When you read about what heaven is made of, signs and wonders begin to make a lot more sense. Let heaven come!

"This is what I will do in the last days—I will pour out my Spirit on everybody and cause your sons and daughters to prophesy, and your young men will see visions, and your old men will experience dreams from God. The Holy Spirit will come upon all my servants, men and women alike, and they will prophesy. I will reveal startling signs and wonders in the sky above and mighty miracles on the earth below. Blood and fire and pillars of clouds will appear. For the sun will be turned dark and the moon blood-red before that great and awesome appearance of the day of the Lord. But everyone who calls on the name of the Lord will be saved." (Acts 2:17-21 TPT)

"And the apostles went out announcing the good news everywhere, as the Lord himself consistently worked with them, validating the message they preached with miracle-signs that accompanied them!" (Mark 16:20 TPT)

I highly recommend Brian Guerin's book titled, *God of Wonders* for an in-depth look on the topic. More signs and wonders will crack open in your life as you read it.

Personal Encounter:

On January 12, 2017, which happened to be my birthday, I experienced the lightnings of God for the first time. The Glory of the Lord began moving on me and I was caught up in a trance. I was running and racing past all of these beautiful bridal veils that hung like flowing curtains.

Then I was pulled into a Throne Room encounter, just likes Revelation chapter 4 talks about the flashes of lightening around the Throne of God. I saw lightning coming from the heavenlies, and as it would hit me, my whole body would jolt uncontrollably as if electrocuted by Glory. As intense as this sounds, it was such a special heavenly encounter.

I then saw angels standing around me and I was given a

white stone with a name written on it. (I don't feel at liberty to reveal the name.) I saw prophetic visions of future times of ministry that I will do for Jesus in advancing His Kingdom. He said to me, "In order to freely give, you must freely receive." I had the sensation of the Glory of God entering into every cell of my body. It was so glorious. For about two hours, I laid there experiencing the ecstasy of His Glory completely love drunk. Heaven was imparting to me what I need for all that the Lord desires to accomplish through my life.

Activation Prayer:

"I pray that the light of God will illuminate the eyes of your imagination, flooding you with light, until you experience the full revelation of the hope of his calling—that is, the wealth of God's glorious inheritances that he finds in us, his holy ones! I pray that you will continually experience the immeasurable greatness of God's power made available to you through faith. Then your lives will be an advertisement of this immense power as it works through you! This is the mighty power." (Ephesians 1:18-19 TPT)

Questions to Ask Jesus:

Jesus, can You give me fresh encounters with You? What do You want to show me?

_____

_____

_____

_____

_____

"Someone living on an entirely human level rejects the revelations of God's Spirit, for they make no sense to him. He can't understand the revelations of the Spirit because they are only discovered by the illumination of the Spirit." (1 Corinthians 2:14 TPT)

"The eyes of your spirit allow revelation-light to enter into your being. When your heart is open the light floods in. When your heart is hard and closed, the light cannot penetrate and darkness takes its place. Open your heart and consider my words. Watch out that you do not mistake your opinions for revelation-light!" (Luke 11:34-35 TPT)

Chapter Nine

ADORNING HIS BRIDE

"*P*hysical manifestations of adorning from God mark us in the Bridal Company." (Delane Morin) To adorn means to decorate or add beauty to. Ladies, we often do this by wearing jewelry or other accessories to accent our clothing. Yet did you realize that Christ is adorning us as His Bride? He not only provides for His Bride, but adorns her with beautiful jewels and provisions.

"For he enjoys his faithful lovers. He adorns the humble with his beauty and he loves to give them the victory." (Psalm 149:4 TPT)

Think about how brides are adorned today with special necklaces and earrings, how they wear their hair in elegant ways. How might we be adorned as the Bride of Christ?

Being Adorned by God

The following passage speaks not only of God's love for us, but about God giving us "increase" and building us with precious stones. They are signs of His love for us.

"'Increase is coming, so enlarge your tent and add extensions to your dwelling. Hold nothing back! Make the tent ropes longer and the pegs stronger. You will increase and spread out in every direction. Your sons and daughters will conquer nations and revitalize desolate cities. Do not fear, for your shame is no more. Do not be embarrassed, for you will not be disgraced. You will forget the inadequacy you felt in your youth and will no longer remember the shame of your widowhood. For your Maker is your husband; his name is Yahweh, Commander of Angel Armies! Your Kinsman-Redeemer is the Holy One of Israel! He has the title Mighty God of All the Earth!

For I, Yahweh, have invited you to come back like a depressed, deserted wife. Like a young wife who has experienced rejection, I am drawing you back to me,' says Yahweh. 'For just a brief moment I deserted you, but with tender feelings of love I will gather you back to me. In a surge of anger, for just the briefest moment, I hid my face from you, but with everlasting kindness, I will show you my cherishing love,' says Yahweh, your Kinsman-Redeemer. 'To me, this is like the time when I vowed that the waters of Noah's flood would never again cover the earth. Now I vow to you that I will neither be angry with you nor rebuke you. Even if the mountains were to crumble and the hills disappear, my heart of steadfast, faithful love will never leave you, and my covenant of peace with you will never be shaken,' says Yahweh, whose love and compassion will never give up on you.

'You unhappy one, storm-tossed and troubled, I am ready to rebuild you with precious stones and embed your foundation with sapphires. I will make your towers of rubies, your gates of sparkling jewels, and all your walls of precious, delightful stones. All your children will be taught by Yahweh, and great will be their peace and prosperity. You will be established in righteousness. Oppression—be far from them! Fear—be far from them! Yes, terror will not come near you, nor will you be afraid. If anyone dares to stir up strife against you, it is not from me! Those who challenge you will go down in defeat. See, I am the one who created the craftsman who fans the coals into a fire and forges a weapon fit for its purpose, and I am the one who created the destroyer to destroy. But I promise you, no weapon meant to hurt you will succeed, and you will refute every accusing word spoken against you. This promise is the inheritance of Yahweh's servants, and their vindication is from me,' says Yahweh." (Isaiah 54:2-17 TPT)

What might this adorning look like today?

Provision

In seasons of supernatural provision, I've heard the Lord say to me that He is adorning His Bride. When it comes to His Bride, He spares no expense. He provides for us and gives us supernatural wisdom in stewarding the things He blesses us with. We should apply the same measure of faith in the area of provision as we do for healing or any other miracle. The Lord does not want us worrying. As we seek Him, everything we need is drawn to us.

"This is why I tell you to never be worried about your life, for all that you need will be provided, such as food, water, clothing—everything your body needs. Isn't there more to your life than a meal? Isn't your body more than clothing?

Look at all the birds—do you think they worry about their existence? They don't plant or reap or store up food, yet your heavenly Father provides them each with food. Aren't you much more valuable to your Father than they? So, which one of you by worrying could add anything to your life?

And why would you worry about your clothing? Look at all the beautiful flowers of the field. They don't work or toil, and yet not even Solomon in all his splendor was robed in beauty more than one of these! So if God has clothed the meadow with hay, which is here for such a short time and then dried up and burned, won't he provide for you the clothes you need—even though you live with such little faith?

So then, forsake your worries! Why would you say, 'What will we eat?' or 'What will we drink?' or 'What will we wear?' For that is what the unbelievers chase after. Doesn't your heavenly Father already know the things your bodies require?

So above all, constantly chase after the realm of God's kingdom and the righteousness that proceeds from him. Then all these less important things will be given to you abundantly. Refuse to worry about tomorrow, but deal with each challenge that comes your way, one day at a time. Tomorrow will take care of itself." (Matthew 6:25-34 TPT)

Wealth

It is the brilliant Glory of Jesus that lights up all of heaven, and wealth is attracted to the King of Glory. As we become one with Jesus, the holy lamb of God and our Bridegroom King, everything that we need is attracted to us. The wealth of nations comes.

"The twelve gates are twelve pearls—each gate made of one pearl. And the street of the city was pure gold, clear as crystal. I saw no temple in the city, for its temple is the Lord God, the Almighty, and the Lamb. The city has no need for the sun or moon to shine, for the glory of God is its light, and its lamp is the Lamb. The people will walk by its light and the kings of the earth will bring their wealth into it." (Revelation 22:21-24 TPT)

Beautiful Character

While I believe He will clothe us with robes more beautiful than we can imagine, our Bridegroom cares more about the beauty of our hearts and spirit. He is adorning us with a heart like His.

"Let your true beauty come from your inner personality, not a focus on the external. For lasting beauty comes from a gentle and peaceful spirit, which is precious in God's sight and is much more important than the outward adornment of elaborate hair, jewelry, and fine clothes." (1 Peter 3:3-4 TPT)

Remember the fruit of His Spirit: love, joy, peace, patience, kindness, goodness, gentleness, and self-control. These adornments are beautiful to our Bridegroom!

Personal Encounter:

I had a heavenly encounter with Jesus in a fun place that I had never seen or heard of before. This was not the treasury room, but carried the same measure of wealth and provision for God's people.

Jesus stood next to me and said, "Welcome to His Riches in Glory." I was in awe. There appeared to be everything needed for people to fulfill their calling on the earth—from the largest thing like deeds to property to the very small things that most people would think carried no significance. Everything we need is available there, in Glory.

This encounter raised my level of faith for provision and the adorning of the Bride of Christ. I began praying for people, when led by Holy Spirit, and supernatural provision would come from the Lord.

"I am convinced that my God will fully satisfy every need you have, for I have seen the abundant riches of glory revealed to me through the Anointed One, Jesus Christ!" (Philippians 4:19 TPT)

———

Activation Prayer:

Jesus, thank You for Your overwhelming love for me. I ask that You raise my level of faith in the area of wealth and provision. Bless me with wisdom to steward all of the ways Your adorning me. I thank You that everything I need is found in knowing You, Jesus, my Bridegroom King. Amen.

"Everything we could ever need for life and godliness has already been deposited in us by his divine power. For all this was lavished upon us through the rich experience of knowing him who has called us by name and invited us to come to him through a glorious manifestation of his goodness. As a result of this, he has given you magnificent promises that are beyond all price, so that through the power of these tremendous promises you can experience partnership with the divine nature, by which you have escaped the corrupt desires that are of the world." (2 Peter 1:3-4 TPT)

Question to Ask Jesus:

Jesus, will You show me the ways that You are adorning me as Your Bride in this season of my life?

_____

_____

_____

_____

_____

Chapter Ten

ADVANCING THE KINGDOM OF OUR BELOVED

*J*esus reveals Kingdom secrets to His Bride. He is King of kings and He came to establish and advance His Kingdom, the highest Kingdom of all. "He explained, 'You've been given the intimate experience of insight into the hidden truths and mysteries of the realm of heaven's kingdom, but they have not. For everyone who listens with an open heart will receive progressively more revelation until he has more than enough. But those who don't listen with an open, teachable heart, even the understanding that they think they have will be taken from them. That's why I teach the people using parables, because they think they're looking for truth, yet because their hearts are unteachable, they never discover it.

Although they will listen to me, they never fully perceive the message I speak. The prophecy of Isaiah describes them perfectly: Although they listen carefully to everything I speak, they don't understand a thing I say. They look and pretend to see, but the eyes of their hearts are closed. Their minds are dull and slow to perceive, their ears are plugged and are hard of hearing, and they have deliberately shut their eyes to the truth. Otherwise they would open their eyes to see, and open their ears to hear, and open their minds to understand. Then they would turn to me and let me instantly heal them. But your eyes are privileged, for they see. Delighted are your ears, for they are open to hear all these things.'" (Matthew 13:11-16 TPT)

As His Bride, we inherit the family business, our Father's business. We are empowered by Holy Spirit to be a witness to the world that God is real. We are to find the lost Bride in the world and introduce her to a Bridegroom King that can satisfy like no other.

Commissioned to Advance our Family's Kingdom

We have literally become the highest ranking royalty on the earth because we are seated in heavenly places with Christ (Ephesians 2:6). Our position becomes Kings/Queens and Priests/Priestesses. We have been given the authority of Christ and have been commissioned to advance His Kingdom throughout the earth (Mark 16:15-20).

For many years the reality of the Kingdom was hidden from me. When I started discovering the Kingdom realm, I felt like I had been bamboozled all along. How is it that no one ever taught me about the Kingdom? It had to be revealed and unveiled for me to see.

The Kingdom is what Jesus taught about most. He said, "Seek FIRST the Kingdom of God and His righteousness and all these things shall be added to you" (Matthew 6:33, emphasis added). It doesn't matter what area of society you work in or live in, you are commissioned to advance God's Kingdom there. Jesus has given us the Keys to His Kingdom to fully operate in His ways with Kingdom authority and power (Matthew 16:19).

The Gift of Childlike Faith

One of the greatest gifts is childlike faith. It takes humility and purity to fully step into it. You can't access the Bridal realm of the Kingdom through legalism and religion; childlike faith gives us access.

Childlike faith does not feel the need to complicate things. It is full of joy, awe, wonder, and exploration. There is a simplicity in looking into the Word and truly believing what it says. Sometimes God uses the "foolish things to confound the wise" (1 Corinthians 1:27). In childlike faith, our intimacy and worship to our Bridegroom King comes with ease. I would rather error on the side of childlike faith than error on the side of legalism and unbelief.

"Learn this well: Unless you dramatically change your way of thinking and become teachable, and learn about heaven's kingdom realm with the wide-eyed wonder of a child, you will never be able to enter in. Whoever continually humbles himself to become like this gentle child is the greatest one in heaven's kingdom realm." (Matthew 18:3-4 TPT)

"'My thoughts are nothing like your thoughts,' says the LORD. 'And my ways are far beyond anything you could imagine. For just as the heavens are higher than the earth, so my ways are higher than your ways and my thoughts higher than your thoughts.'" (Isaiah 55:8-9 NLT)

Rise Up and Advance

Rise up and take your place in the Kingdom of God. No longer do you have to live below what has been given to you in your inheritance as a child of God and the Bride of Christ! "For the Kingdom realm of God comes with power, not simply impressive words" (1 Corinthians 4:20 TPT). You MUST seek to understand everything that you rightfully own in the Kingdom and live in the health, wealth, authority, power, and abundance that Jesus died for you to possess. Explore the Kingdom through the Word of God for yourself. The

Kingdom of God should be more real to you than anything else.

As you embark on this journey of Advancing the Kingdom of your Beloved Jesus, there are a few things to be in prayer about:

1. "Seek FIRST the Kingdom of God and His righteousness and all these things shall be added to you" (Matthew 6:33, emphasis added). Everything that we need in life can be found in our pursuit of the Kingdom of God and His righteousness that Jesus came to establish on the earth.

2. Be prepared to change your thinking to be Kingdom focused. "Stop imitating the ideals and opinions of the culture around you, but be inwardly transformed by the Holy Spirit through a total reformation of how you think. This will empower you to discern God's will as you live a beautiful life, satisfying and perfect in his eyes" (Romans 12:2 TPT).

3. Know you have the power to bring heavenly healing and power here to earth. "And as you go, preach this message: 'Heaven's kingdom realm is accessible, close enough to touch.' You must continually bring healing to lepers and to those who are sick, and make it your habit to break off the demonic presence from people, and raise the dead back to life. Freely you have received the power of the kingdom, so freely release it to others" (Matthew 10:7-8 TPT).

4. Let your Husband, Jesus, be your model. "I tell you this timeless truth: The person who follows me in faith, believing in me, will do the same mighty

miracles that I do—even greater miracles than these because I go to be with my Father! For I will do whatever you ask me to do when you ask me in my name. And that is how the Son will show what the Father is really like and bring glory to him. Ask me anything in my name, and I will do it for you!" (John 14:12-14 TPT).

So many are searching for a new way of life and freedom from the horrors of this world. You have the answer. Share the Good News and welcome them into the Kingdom. Rise up and take your place in the Kingdom! Spread the message of the Bridegroom King Jesus all over the world.

"And the Apostles went out announcing the Good News everywhere, as the Lord himself consistently worked with them, validating the message they preached with miracle-signs that accompanied them!" (Mark 16:20 TPT)

Personal Encounter:

When I first started stepping out to release the power of the Kingdom while praying for healing miracles, the Lord greatly encouraged me. I had this thought in my head that "one day" in the future, it would be easier to fulfill the "calling to the nations" on my life and move consistently in the power of the Kingdom. Jesus showed me that every word He has ever spoken over me is fully active *now*, that I didn't have to wait for the future. Prophetic words speak to identity, not just things that we do in the future.

I will never forget one of the first times Jesus gave me a word of knowledge for a stranger. I was driving my kids home from school and I heard a word of knowledge as I passed by some construction guys standing across the street from my house. I parked the car and juggled bags and kids, getting everything inside. I heard it again: "sciatic nerve damage." I saw a vision of a red sweatshirt. I made a PB&J sandwich for my toddler, who was screaming in tears and swinging around my ankle. I then changed my baby boy's diaper. I heard the Lord again.

After getting the kids settled, I decided to take out the trash. My husband was home, so I went outside to investigate what Jesus was saying. My heart raced because I felt the Lord so strongly, but I was a little scared, to be honest. I mustered up the strength to cross the street and approach the strangers.

"Does one of you have sciatic nerve damage, by any chance?" They all responded, "No."

I replied, "Are you sure? My husband and I are in ministry and I love praying for people to receive healing miracles from Jesus." I was looking at the man in the red sweatshirt. He now changed his answer and said, "Well, actually, I've had a couple of surgeries because of sciatic nerve damage and I'm still in pain." He allowed me to pray with him and release the love of God over him. Such a powerful moment.

This situation encouraged me to believe for the miraculous in everyday life. I learned that I didn't have to wait to go to the nations to fulfill my calling. I just have to walk yielded to my love, Jesus, in the advancing of His Kingdom. We have since seen Jesus heal more people than we could record. It is such a joy to partner with heaven to release the Kingdom, to see people surrender their lives to Jesus and find healing and freedom.

Activation Prayer:

Jesus, remove any legalistic mindsets or influences from religious spirits. Bless me with childlike faith to explore the realities of Your Kingdom. Baptize me in Your Spirit so that I can be empowered to advance Your Kingdom on the earth with power. Amen.

Question to Ask Jesus:

Jesus, can You reveal the truths and secrets of the Kingdom to me? (Matthew 13:11)

_____

_____

_____

_____

_____

*For more insight on the Kingdom of God, I highly recommend *When Heaven Invades Earth* by Bill Johnson. *Power to Heal: Keys to Activating God's Healing Power in Your Life* by Randy Clark is another incredible resource.

Chapter Eleven

MARRIED TO THE KING OF ANGEL ARMIES

"*L*ook! It is the king's marriage carriage. The love seat surrounded by sixty champions, the mightiest of Israel's host, are like pillars of protection. They are angelic warriors standing ready with swords to defend the king and his fiancée from every terror of the night. The king made this mercy seat for himself out of the finest wood that will not decay. Pillars of smoke, like silver mist—a canopy of golden glory dwells above it. The place where they sit together is sprinkled with crimson. Love and mercy cover this carriage, blanketing his tabernacle throne. The king himself has made it for those who will become his bride." (Song of Songs 3:7-10 TPT)

What a beautiful and powerful picture of how the angel armies accompany the Bride! This is our reality married to the King of Angel Armies. He sends His messengers to accompany us. You have angels serving and helping you daily whether you realize it or not.

"For your Creator will be your husband; the Lord of Heaven's Armies is his name! He is your Redeemer, the Holy One of Israel, the God of all the earth." (Isaiah 54:5 NLT)

Becoming Aware of Angelic Activity

We are one with the Lord. We are His Bride. Jesus is King

of Angel Armies. As we experience more and more of Him in the Bridal realm of encounter, our awareness of angelic activity increases. I have recognized more angelic activity in my life than ever before, as Jesus has been appearing to me as the Bridegroom. I share some stories below. You, too, are being awakened to a greater reality of angels that are very present to minister to and help you as His Bride.

Angels are mentioned 296 times in the Bible. There is much importance to their part of assisting the Bride of Christ. Angels appear all throughout the Bible bringing messages from God, freedom, encouragement, prophecy, words of knowledge, direction, and so much more. Angels were even present to help Jesus during His ministry. There are so many stories of angels showing up in Scripture, more than I have space to share. Here are a few of my favorites to study if you feel led: Ezekiel 1, Luke 1, Isaiah 6, Revelation 4, Acts 10:1-6, and Acts 12:5-17.

"Are not all the angels ministering spirits sent out [by God] to serve (accompany, protect) those who will inherit salvation? [Of course they are!]" (Hebrews 1:14 AMP)

Angel Headquarters

My son, Zane, started having dreams and visions of Jesus and angels at age four. I am continually blown away by what he sees. He has had a couple of dreams where Jesus took him to the angel headquarters in heaven. He explains Jesus taking him up through space, then to what looks like a big palace covered in feathers that could change rainbow colors. The feathers had eyes on them. He said it was really cool because the eyes on the feathers were like the security cameras of the palace. He saw all kinds of angels.

Jesus took him into a fighting room full of weapons. Jesus was teaching him how to fight bad guys that looked like bad aliens. He set up figures for Zane to practice with. Then Jesus took him on a tour of the rest of the headquarters. I was so in awe.

When my son had his first dream about this heavenly place, I had never read him Scriptures of what angels specifically look like. He had no idea previously that there really are angels with eyes all over their feathers and bodies (Ezekiel 10:12-14, Revelation 4:6-9). I came across a book in which a minister describes their heavenly encounter at the Archangel Michael's Headquarters, and it looks exactly as Zane described. It is mind blowing. Additionally, some personal breakthrough happened in Zane's life after these dreams. He stopped having nightmares and was no longer afraid of the dark.

Stairwell Ladder into the Sky

There are a couple of times in Scripture where a secret stairwell or ladder in the sky is mentioned and angels ascend and descend upon it.

"At sundown he arrived at a good place to set up camp and stopped there for the night. Jacob found a stone to rest his head against and lay down to sleep. As he slept, he dreamed of a stairway that reached from the earth up to heaven. And he saw the angels of God going up and down the stairway. At the top of the stairway stood the Lord, and he said, 'I am the Lord, the God of your grandfather Abraham, and the God of your father, Isaac.

The ground you are lying on belongs to you. I am giving it to you and your descendants. Your descendants will be as numerous as the dust of the earth! They will spread out in all directions—to the west and the east, to the north and the south. And all the families of the earth will be blessed through you and your descendants. What's more, I am with you, and I will protect you wherever you go. One day I will bring you back to this land. I will not leave you until I have finished giving you everything I have promised you.'" (Genesis 28:11-15 NLT)

Below, Jesus is speaking to one of His disciples, prophesying that he would see the angels of the Lord coming and going to and from heaven upon Him. We as disciples, as the Bride, can see and encounter angels coming and going.

"I prophesy to you eternal truth: From now on you all will see an open heaven and gaze upon the Son of Man like a stairway reaching into the sky with the messengers of God climbing up and down upon him!" (John 1:51 TPT)

Finally, we see the Bride of Christ hidden within that same heavenly stairwell. We, as the Bride, have a place with the Lord. He gives us heavenly access. There is a sublime sanctuary that we can experience with Him, and the angels of the Lord are present to assist us in fulfilling His will.

"For you are my dove, hidden in the split-open rock. It was I who took you and hid you up high in the secret stairway of the sky. Let me see your radiant face and hear your sweet voice. How beautiful your eyes of worship and lovely your voice in prayer." (Song of Songs 2:14 TPT)

When Angels Show Up

It was very common in the Bible for angels to show up and deliver messages from God. Today, there seems to be not much talk of them. I am personally so thankful for their supernatural help in my life.

There are several indicators that angels are on the scene: feathers popping out of thin air, lights zipping around the room (sometimes orb shaped), an increased presence of glory, or a sensation of wind from wings, just to name a few. They appear in dreams, visions, and trances, and sometimes you can see their frame outlined right in front of you. My point in sharing these things is to open up your faith in knowing that angels show up in several ways. You may even speak to one unaware. "And show hospitality to strangers, for they may be angels from God showing up as your guests." (Hebrews 13:2 TPT)

I love this visual of our Bridegroom King Lover Jesus as King of Angel Armies. If you read the following verses slow enough with an open heart, you can visually see the Scripture and may slip into an encounter with Him. This is what the Word of God looks like when He, Jesus, rides in on your behalf with all of heaven behind Him.

"Then I saw heaven opened, and suddenly a white horse appeared. The name of the one riding it was Faithful and True, and with pure righteousness he judges and rides to battle. He wore many regal crowns, and his eyes were flashing like flames of fire. He had a secret name inscribed on him that's known only to himself. He wore a robe dipped in blood, and his title is called the Word of God. Following him on white horses were the armies of heaven, wearing white fine linen, pure and bright. A sharp sword came from his mouth with which to conquer the nations, and he will shepherd them with an iron scepter. He will trample out the wine in the winepress of the wrath of God. On his robe and on his thigh he had inscribed a name: King of kings and Lord of lords." (Revelation 19:11-16 TPT)

Personal Encounters:

One night, I had an angel help me get breakthrough from violent warfare attacks that I was dealing with. I had just finished a 40 day liquids fast. I was thinking that I would start feeling better in my body upon completion of the fast. However, I experienced some crazy attacks of sickness in my body from lack of nutrition on the fast. I was also fighting aggressive assaults in the spirit at night. The Lord encouraged me that He too suffered warfare after His 40 day fast and that He would help me through.

These attacks were happening every night for about 10 days straight, so I asked an intercessor friend of mine to pray with me. After that prayer, the assaults stopped, but I was still running in my dreams, fearful of being attacked again. The enemy was trying to find, track, and trace me. I'm so thankful that the Lord sent an angel to help.

When I fell asleep, someone was pulling my foot and waking me up as I was running scared in my sleep. I woke up and at first thought that one of my kids was out of bed messing with me. This continued to happen and I was quickened to know that an angel was there helping me fight.

In my dream, German shepherds were trying to find me and sniff me out on a field with others lined up. The dog traced me and found me signaling the enemy that I was caught. A woman came to me with an evil smile and told me to go in the building and everything was going to be ok. I felt trapped. Immediately, demonic men tried to run in and rape me. I closed and locked the door in time. On my knees, facing the doorknob, I sunk my fingernails into the lock and held it tight to keep it closed. Throughout the dream, an angel was with me continuing to tug at my foot. Even though I was in a war, I felt the peace and presence of God in my room. As I woke up, I heard the angel audibly say, "Good, it stuck."

I am so thankful for breakthrough from the warfare. I have not been assaulted at night in my dreams since. This is a big deal since I've dealt with warfare in my dreams from the time I was a child. You can read more about my life story in the last section of this book. I shared the vulnerability of this experience in hope that you might be encouraged and have more faith in the assistance of heaven's armies in your life.

Activation Prayer:

Lord, open my eyes so that I can see, just as You opened the eyes of Elisha's servant to see heaven's armies. Lord, help me to be aware of and partner with heaven. Amen. "'Don't be afraid!' Elisha told him. 'For there are more on our side than on theirs!' Then Elisha prayed, 'O Lord, open his eyes and let him see!' The Lord opened the young man's eyes, and when he looked up, he saw that the hillside around Elisha was filled with horses and chariots of fire." (2 Kings 6:16-17 NLT)

Question to Ask Jesus:

Lord, can You show me a time in my life when You sent angelic help to me?

_____
_____
_____
_____
_____

*For a more in-depth study on angels, I highly recommend *Angel Armies – Releasing the Warriors of Heaven* by Tim Sheets

Chapter Twelve

OUR HUSBAND IS KING OF GLORY

"*S*o wake up, you living gateways! Lift up your heads, you ageless doors of destiny! Welcome the Glory-King who is about to come through you! You ask, 'Who is this Glory-King?' It is the Lord, armed and ready for battle, the Mighty One, invincible in every way! So wake up you living gateways, and rejoice! Fling wide open, you forever-doors of destiny! Here He comes; the Glory-King is ready to come in! You ask, 'Who is this Glory-King?' He's the Lord of Victory, armed and ready for battle, The Mighty One, invincible Commander of heaven's hosts! Yes, He is the Glory-King!" (Psalm 24:7-10 TPT)

The King of Glory, your Husband Jesus, is coming through your life in greater measures. There are several manifestations of His glory, and as you step into Bridal Encounters with Him, you will experience more glory than ever before. You may experience sensations like fire, rain, wind, whirlwind, a cloud, weighty glory, or drunken glory full of laughter and joy, and that's just to name a few.

We do not seek the manifestation, but we seek our Beloved Jesus and the glory comes with Him. He is King of Glory. I don't care how He comes, I just want to be with Him, right in the middle of whatever He is doing and with Him wherever He is. I love the way He moves. I'm obsessed with Him! Encountering the glory of God is my favorite thing to do. There is simply no experience that tops it!

"And so the Living Expression became a man and lived among us! And we gazed upon the splendor of his glory, the glory of the One and Only who came from the Father overflowing with tender mercy and truth!" (John 1:14 TPT)

"Instead, we continually speak of this wonderful wisdom that comes from God, hidden before now in a mystery. It is his secret plan, destined before the ages, to bring us into glory. None of the rulers of this present world order understood it, for if they had, they never would have crucified the Lord of shining glory. This is why the Scriptures say: 'Things never discovered or heard of before, things beyond our ability to imagine these are the many things God has in store for all his lovers.' But God now unveils these profound realities to us by the Spirit. Yes, he has revealed to us his inmost heart and deepest mysteries through the Holy Spirit, who constantly explores all things." (1 Corinthians 2:7-10 TPT)

The Glory Cloud

The most brilliant manifestation of the glory that I have ever witnessed in person took place in March of 2018 at our church. A cloud of glory appeared. It looked as if there were clouds in the ceiling over the platform. We do not own a smoke machine and there is no natural explanation for what we saw. Glory was swirling with diamond dust and little feathers. As you moved your hands through it, you would be covered in glory. We were in awe and childlike wonder. Laughing, screaming, worshiping Jesus. The cloud would increase as we worshipped the Lord. We have seen the Glory Cloud appear a couple of times and I really have no adequate words to explain it. Every once in a while, the cloud appears. I began studying

"Cloud of Glory" in Scripture and found that there are records of the glory appearing in this manner throughout the Bible. Then I found videos of the glory cloud appearing at Bethel Church in Redding, California, a few years ago.

Now, all of this may be a little bit of a stretch for some people who have never witnessed something like this before, but all I can say is that we want God to show up however He wants to. We try not to control or limit the moving of His presence and glory. When the King of Glory shows up, glory and signs and wonders come with Him. At the time of writing this book, we are just a small church plant of about 300 people. We are so humbled by the way that Jesus, King of Glory, shows up. We are forever thankful to Him.

"Who is ascending from the wilderness in the pillar of the glory cloud? He is fragrant with the anointing oils of myrrh and frankincense–more fragrant than all the spices of the merchant." (Song of Songs 3:6 TPT)

We are Glory Carriers

Not only does God reveal His glory to us, but we were created to be Glory Carriers on the earth. We are the modern day walking and breathing "Ark of the Covenant," revealing His glory to those around us.

"...God is transforming each one of you into the Holy of Holies, his dwelling place, through the power of the Holy Spirit living in you!" (Ephesians 2:22 TPT)

"Bring me everyone who is called by my name, the ones I created to experience my glory. I myself formed them to be who they are and made them for my glory." (Isaiah 43:7 TPT)

"And doesn't he also have the right to release the revelation of the wealth of his glory to his vessels of mercy, whom God prepared beforehand to receive his glory? Even for us, whether we are Jews or non-Jews, we are those he has called to experience his glory." (Romans 9:23-24 TPT)

"For I know your power and presence shines on all your lovers. Your glory always hovers over all who bow low before you." (Psalm 85:9 TPT)

He Invites Us into Glory Encounters with Him

The disciples who walked the closest to the Lord were taken into glorious heavenly experiences with Jesus. I want to walk so close with Jesus that He can trust me enough to bring me into places of His glory with Him.

"After six days, Jesus took Peter and the two brothers, Jacob and John, and hiked up a high mountain to be alone. And Jesus' appearance was dramatically altered, for he was transfigured before their very eyes! His clothing sparkled and became glistening white—whiter than any bleach in the world could make them. Then suddenly, right in front of them, Moses and Elijah appeared, and they spoke with Jesus. Peter blurted out, 'Beautiful Teacher, this is so amazing to see the three of you together! Why don't we stay here and set up three shelters: one for you, one for Moses, and one for Elijah?' (For all of the disciples were in total fear, and Peter didn't have a clue what to say.) Just then, a radiant cloud began to spread over them, enveloping them all. And God's voice suddenly spoke from the cloud, saying, 'This is my most dearly loved Son—always listen to him!' Suddenly, when they looked around, the disciples saw only Jesus, for Moses and Elijah had faded away." (Mark 9:2-8 TPT)

Jesus is still inviting us into glory encounters with Him. There is more available for you to experience with Him than you have ever encountered. As you are spending time in the glory, you should start looking and sounding more and more like Him. The glory transforms us more and more into His image (2 Corinthians 3:16-18). RIGHT NOW there is an invitation....

"Draw me into your heart. We will run away together into the King's cloud-filled chamber." (Song of Songs 1:4 TPT)
How will you respond to His invitation to draw near?

You are His Bride

Jesus has called you as His precious Bride. You are valuable to Him and He is pursuing you, inviting you into deeper intimacy with Him. He wants to enter into a marriage covenant with you, one in which He will transform you as you are in divine union with Him. He is making you pure, holy, beautiful. He is adorning you with precious stones and jewels.

Your Bridegroom has given you His name, along with the power and authority that it holds. Use it to bring about His Kingdom here on earth. Heal sicknesses, set people free from their sins and oppression, reveal heaven as it is here right now. Become more aware of His angels' activities among us.

But most importantly, take the time to recognize His presence in your life and to gaze into His lovely face. Draw close to your Husband, dear one, and let Him take you to His chamber and love you.

Personal Encounter:

The most intense glory encounter of my life was at a conference in February of 2018. The electric glory of God was so strong that I thought I was going to die. I was being electrocuted with the lightnings of His glory, while seeing glimpses of Jesus coming closer and closer. I couldn't help it but to scream in worship. I never knew that it was possible to experience what was happening to me. I wanted the glory to slightly lift because of the intensity, but at the same time, I wanted more.

There was a precious woman that tried to come pray with me. She didn't understand what was going on and was trying to "cast Holy Spirit" out of me. Bless her heart. (Side Note: If you're not careful, you can find yourself busy with false discernment and judging others, while Jesus passes you by. Never judge someone who is experiencing God. You don't know what they've been through to worship Him with the measure of intensity that they do.) I kindly explained to her, while completely inebriated with drunken glory, "You don't understand. It's the glory. It's the glory. It's the glory!" The whole room was exploding with glory and sounds of revival. What a joy to be present on that day. There is so much power and beauty when gathering together in a corporate setting of hungry people... Jesus, King of Glory comes!

Activation Prayer:

Lord, "show me Your glory" (Exodus 33:13-19)! King of Glory, come! Jesus, be a wall of fire around me and pour out Your glory on me (Zechariah 2:5). Lord, give me wisdom in carrying Your glory on the earth. Would You bless me with a greater hunger for You? I want to know You more intimately, Jesus, King of Glory! Amen.

Question to Ask Jesus:

Jesus, what facets of Your glory are You bringing into my life now?

_____

_____

_____

_____

_____

"The source of revelation knowledge is found as you fall down in surrender before the Lord. Don't expect to see the shekinah glory until the Lord sees your humility." (Proverbs 15:33 TPT)

FREE EXCERPT FROM
FIGHTING FOR YOUR PURPOSE

BY SULA SKILES

THE FOLLOWING PAGES INCLUDE MY TRAUMATIC LIFE STORY AND HOW
JESUS REACHED ME IN MY DARKEST PLACES. I BELIEVE THAT HE WILL DO THE
SAME FOR YOU.

My earliest memories in life are of sexual abuse. I remember being pushed under heavy comforters, large mouths covering my little toddler lips, large body parts violating my little body parts, and being suffocated. It was so hard to breathe. I would scream inside, but nothing came out. I had so much fear because I remember someone threatening me not to tell, or else. This treatment was my "normal." I don't remember anything before that. I was 18 months old when sexual violation and abuse started. It was only the beginning of a lifetime of horrible events sewn together like a patchwork quilt depicting a dark, traumatic nightmare almost too terrible to be true.

My mom was a very hard-working young woman. She had me at age 19 and was determined to be successful in life. She was in school preparing for her master's degree and doing the best that she could as a single mom. My sexual abuse occurred while being watched by a trusted couple who were friends and had a daughter a year-and-a-half older than me. One day, my mom was tickling me and did a raspberry on my belly, making that funny sound. We were laughing and having fun, so I said to her, "Mommy, do that down here," pointing to my private part. She told me, "We don't do that." I insisted, "Yeah, put your mouth down here." She then started asking me questions and was horrified by what she discovered. This is how my mom remembers finding out that her 3-year-old baby girl was being molested by the very people she trusted to care for me.

She immediately called the police and child protective

services to make a report and start an investigation. She was told to never speak to that family again because the investigation was going to get messy. I started seeing a children's therapist. Her office was in an older Victorian-style building. I remember staring at the vintage white walls in the waiting area, feeling uncomfortable and just wanting to get it over with. The therapist had red, frizzy, curly hair and was soft and round in stature. I loved playing with the sand box she had in her office. She had a bookshelf of little people, buildings, trees, and cars. Sometimes I got to add water to my sand world creations. I was more concerned with playing than talking. I do remember her attempting a type of hypnosis: I was to relax and envision a safe, happy place. I still remember a vision from one of those sessions of a park waterfall that was very peaceful and everything was purple. Boy, do I wish that purple vision could have really kept me safe from harm, but it didn't. I was a difficult child due to the abuse I endured and the absence of a father.

I loved my mama. I would always scoop my arm through hers every time we walked anywhere. I remember always wanting to sleep with her. It was extremely hard when I had to transition to being a big girl and sleep in my own bed. Demons attacked me and sexually abused me when I slept by myself. I had a major fear of being left alone at night because that's when most of the sexual abuse previously occurred. I had to talk myself into going to sleep because almost every time I shut my eyes, horror met me again.

My Safety Mask of Lies

I had lots of friends as a kid, but at the same time, I felt very alone. From a very early age, I developed a delusional fantasy world. It was my defense mechanism. I just wanted to fit in to what I thought was normal. I wanted to forget how my life began, tangled in sexual perversion. I did a lot of "make-believe." Acting was one of my favorite things to do. I would put together dances and comedic plays whenever friends came over and would have the adults watch. There was something about making people laugh that made me feel good about myself. The toys and activities I liked usually involved acting and make-believe. I liked to make up characters because I could be anyone I wanted to.

Unfortunately, I took that to the extreme throughout my life and developed a serious lying problem. I was smiling on the outside and tormented on the inside. This made it very difficult for my mom or anyone to help me with the inward demons I fought. It was hard to decipher what was true and what was part of my dysfunctional mindset. My make-believe, delusions, and lies made me feel safe. If no one could find the real me inside, maybe they couldn't hurt me. I was always searching for something and someone to make sense of my life.

Strange Things Happening

As a young girl, there was a series of strange things that happened spiritually. I would know things before they happened. For example, one time I threw a temper tantrum because I couldn't leave the house without being dressed head to toe like Dorothy from *The Wizard of Oz*. That day, we went to pick up my Grandma Ruth from the airport, and when she saw me, she freaked out. When we got home, she made my mom take pictures of me opening the present Grandma brought me. I unwrapped the gift and it was a doll, and guess what she was wearing. The exact same outfit I had on. The shoes, socks, dress, and even our hair was the same.

Another strange moment was when my mom and her boyfriend carried me asleep into the horse race track. I repeated a number a couple of times as I was sleeping in his arms. My mom suggested that he bet on the horse with the number I was mumbling. He looked up the horse and found that horse was always a loser, so he didn't bet on it. Guess which horse won. That's right, the underdog won that day. If he would have bet on that horse, he would have won a lot of money. He tried asking me for a number every time he went to the track after that, but I never knew the winning horse's number again.

I always knew there was something different about me. There were several other situations like the examples I mentioned. It sounds like it was a pretty cool thing to experience, but it wasn't. These strange happenings isolated me more from others, because when I tried talking to people about it, they never really understood. In fact, I often felt misunderstood. My family wasn't religious in any way. We never regularly went to church, a mosque, a temple, or anything religious. We attended Easter or Christmas services with a friend maybe five times, but that's it. Spiritually, things were confusing to me.

Witchcraft

At about age 11, I started getting involved with witchcraft. I consistently read horoscopes and was really interested in anything supernatural. How did I know things before they happened? Maybe I was psychic! I would search at stores for anything to help me find information on WICCA. I considered myself to be a good witch. I even sewed myself a black robe to wear during séances. I would cast spells on people and often attempted to communicate with spirits. This opened a realm of darkness in my life that I wasn't ready for. The nightmares intensified. I had hallucinations and visions of demons trying to choke me while I slept. A recurring nighttime experience was demons coming to touch me and rape me. I was not ready or equipped for the evil that I welcomed into my life through WICCA and Tarot Cards. I became so entangled with negativity that I became suicidal. Not only that, but I developed a deep demonic hatred for my mother. I hated myself and I hated her. For some reason, I blamed her for all of my pain, which was unrealistic. When she became aware of how serious this momentum of hatred was building inside, she took me to therapy again. When the therapist found out I wanted to kill myself and wished my mom dead, as well, she admitted me.

Call Me Crazy

At age twelve, I was institutionalized in a mental hospital psych ward for depression and being suicidal. I was clinically diagnosed with bipolar disorder, which caused several dysfunctional actions and decisions in my life. I remember hopelessly gazing out the window as the dramatics of another patient flailing down the hallway with nurses in pursuit brandishing needles transpired in my peripheral vision. I gazed around the room, numb and emotionless at the insane psych patients, realizing I was now one of them. I remember thinking about how crazy they were, as if my diagnosis of bipolar disorder, along with several other issues, made me any better than them.

After trial medications and medical professionals attempting to help me, in my mind, I concluded that there had to be something more. There had to be someone or something that could break me out of my inward cell of trauma, abuse, and torment. I didn't feel like my life was worth anything. I was searching, and nothing satisfied the huge void I had on the inside.

I quickly learned the system in the psychiatric hospital and how people were able to get out. So, I said everything I thought they wanted to hear and pretended to the best of my ability to play the role of someone "improving" from their condition. Once I was released, I begged my mom to take me off of the bipolar medications. I hated how it made me feel. This taught me that it was better to conceal my craziness. I knew if I talked about the demonic hallucinations or my depression, I would end up back in the hospital, so I kept it all to myself, internalizing more pain.

Abortion One

I was 14 years old when I had my first boyfriend. I thought I was in love and couldn't get enough of being with him. He was a couple of years older than me and lived in the Buena Vista Apartments. Most of my friends lived in that several block radius known as "the BV's."

On my boyfriend's birthday, he took me to one of his friend's apartments across the street and told me that there was one gift that he wanted. He convinced me that I had to give him my virginity. We started drinking, which we usually did when we were together. I didn't even really know what to say, so I didn't say anything. I just did it. I laid there still and quiet. In my head were racing pictures and memories of sexual abuse from the past. I never knew how to tell someone "no" without the fear of something bad happening to me. I wanted to tell him I wasn't ready, that I didn't really like what we were doing, but he was my first boyfriend and I didn't want to disappoint him.

That was the beginning of being convinced almost every time we were together that we should have sex. One day, my mom approached me inquiring why I hadn't asked her to buy me any of my monthly toiletries. I didn't even realize that I had missed my period. I found out I was pregnant and it was decided that I was to get an abortion. So, at 14, I had my first abortion.

Smarty Pants

I always loved school. My high school achievements were one of the few things that I loved about myself. I really excelled in my classes and loved science. I took honors classes and even took a few college courses at the community college while in high school. I was nominated for and attended the National Youth Leadership Forum on Medicine at UCLA. I also had the privilege of going to a science class/program at Stanford for high school students interested in that field. I was able to hide behind good grades and academic honors. Here I was, a social butterfly, doing exceptionally well in school, yet completely broken and hurting on the inside.

Alcohol and Drugs

I didn't know how to feel better about myself. I didn't know how to recover from all of the trauma I had endured. So, I self-medicated. I would take vodka to school in water bottles and go to class drunk. No one ever knew because I hid it all so well. I started doing ecstasy and soon after, found someone who sold acid. The very thing that I thought would take away my pain and numb my tormenting thoughts and feelings only made things worse.

Raped by a Stranger

I met a guy who was over 21 through some friends and saw him as a great opportunity to get free alcohol. I always kept my eyes open for someone to buy me alcohol. I was such a stupid, naïve girl... I thought I was using him for alcohol, and he ended up using me for so much more.

Something about that drink he got for me hit me much harder than expected. I knew my limits and I had my favorites. Strawberry Scisco tasted like candy and I drank it often. But this time, I blacked out. That hadn't happened before. I was able to open my heavy eyelids a couple of times only to see him naked on top of me.

When I snapped out of it, my clothes were off and I knew what had taken place. I had been raped. I felt like I deserved it. This was my second time hanging out with him. I didn't know him. I was more concerned about getting alcohol than about my safety. I obviously never called him again for "free" Strawberry Scisco, because it wasn't really free.

Bisexual?

After being raped, I played with the idea that maybe girls would treat me better than guys. I was part of the girls' volleyball team at school and a few of us spent way too much time together. I didn't actually have a relationship with a girl, but I thought I was bisexual. We drank and did ecstasy together on weekends. It was an escape from reality and became the highlight of my life at the time. Drugs, best friends, partying all night long, and no boys. I was confused and searching for anything and anyone who could make me feel happy, even if it was only for a moment.

Abortion Two

At age 16, I was in a relationship on and off for about a year. I got pregnant and was so scared. I went to the clinic on my high school campus and was actually able to make an appointment for an abortion without parental consent. I hid everything from my family, as usual. The only thing I needed from my boyfriend was a ride home after the procedure. They told me that I would be too drugged up to drive myself. Of course, he was nowhere to be found, so I went alone.

I could tell the doctor was burnt out and had had a busy day. I was crying when he entered the room and he said in an irritated tone of voice, "You are going to have to stop crying. You made this decision. Put your legs up and let's get you in position. I have a lot of patients to see." I was shocked by his statement. It hurt my feelings even more, but I needed him. I needed him to erase my mistake. I was more scared of getting in trouble at the moment than the lifetime of depression and guilt from killing my baby.

This time, I didn't have the cushion of health insurance, so I was awake during the abortion. They didn't even have the decency to cover the trash or bloody instruments before sitting me up. I saw the chunks of flesh and blood in the trash can. Is that my baby? I took time to recover in the waiting room, then lied to the nurse and told her my ride was waiting for me downstairs. No one was waiting for me. My boyfriend was nowhere to be found. The next day, I found him hugged up with another girl and kissing after school. I sunk to an all new low.

Salvation

One of my friends invited me to a youth church service on a Tuesday night. We went and I accepted Jesus into my heart as my Lord and personal Savior. This is what I was searching for all my life. I became almost addicted to being at church. Every time the doors were open, I wanted to be there. I had so much I needed healing and deliverance from. I quickly moved to the altar every time they had a time for prayer at the conclusion of service. My hurts, demons, traumas, and pain were cut off of my life one by one. This new faith and God's love were the only things that actually worked. Nothing else in life helped me. I found my help, my salvation.

There was one Friday night Holy Ghost service in particular that I will never forget. Collapsed across the altar in a heap with tears in my eyes and makeup and mascara running all over my face, the Lord called me into ministry. A majority of the masses of tired and hungry people had already left the church building, gotten into their cars, and driven off in search of any restaurant open late night on a Friday. I had just recently been saved. I still didn't really understand the whole Christianity thing. I attempted to sit myself up and pull my tangled, sweaty, hot hair away from my face and I heard God's voice again.

In the following weeks, people came up to me at different times speaking into my life, saying things like, "You have a purpose." "You've got a calling on your life." "God has an anointing on you for ministry." "God is going to send you to the Nations." What did all of that mean? Surely God had the wrong person! How could He use someone so messed up and broken? I already had more life experiences than most seasoned women in old age, and not the good kind. It was hard for me to believe that God would see anything valuable in me. I had a childhood of sexual abuse, had been raped, was suicidal, and struggled with drugs and alcohol, as well as dysfunctional relationships, and already had two abortions. There was no way I could be used for anything good!

Despite my feelings of unworthiness, I could not deny that He touched me that night and spoke to my heart. Little did I know, the path ahead of me would not be easy. Every time I stepped away from the Truth that set me free, I found myself bound again. I experienced salvation and a God calling, but I still didn't know how to deal with troubles, attacks, and hard times. I didn't yet have the tools and wisdom of how to fight for my purpose. Additionally, there were some legalistic teachings that I was consistently exposed to, which made me feel like I was so unworthy and unholy.

Ex-Boyfriend Murdered

About a year after my second abortion and break up with my ex-boyfriend, I got horrific news—he had been murdered! Someone shot him in the head while he was sleeping in a car. He had a very troubled life. After we broke up, he moved away for a little bit and when he moved back to the area, something was different. He started stealing from several people and ended up in jail. I visited him a couple of times and actually picked him up from his grandma's house and took him to church with me. I connected with the broken boy on the inside and wanted him to experience the same freedom I had. I tried encouraging him and talking to him about God. I had no idea how dangerous his life had become and I couldn't believe that he had been murdered. This added another layer of guilt and shame from having my second abortion. I wondered, "Was I any different from the person who shot him?"

Beginning to Be Used by God

I drew closer and closer to God. I would spend hours in my prayer and Bible study time. I started getting a few opportunities to teach and preach. It was exciting to be used by the Lord. I became aware of gifts and talents within and better understood why there were always "strange things happening" in my life even from childhood and why I was different. Everything about me started making sense. I was attending San Francisco

State University and enjoyed ministering to strangers to and from school, and everywhere I went. One of those strangers became a friend, then a boyfriend, and eventually asked me to marry him.

Raped by Someone I Loved

I was convinced that since we were getting married, it was okay to have sex. What a lie! I started feeling convicted and had a conversation with my fiancé that I had decided to wait until we were married to have sex again. He didn't really like that, but accepted my decision.

Soon after that conversation, I discovered that he had a porn addiction. I found VHS videos of porn all over his room. I confronted him about it. After that discovery, I started distancing myself from him.

One day, I came to his house to talk, and as we sat on his bed, something changed in him. He ripped off my clothes, held me down, and said, "Your body is mine. You belong to me. I can have you whenever I want you." He raped me. This was even worse than being raped by a stranger because I loved him. This was the person I thought I was going to marry. I was devastated and confused. I was trying to live for God. How could this happen to me? I was lost, angry, and extremely alone. The trauma caused me to blame God and run from Him instead of running to Him.

Stripper

Soon after that, my living situation changed. I felt like I had nowhere to go. I was desperate and had no money. So, I did what many girls in the state of California do when they feel rejected, hopeless, and homeless... I became a stripper. I found a strip club a long drive away from where I lived. It was a "no contact" all-nude strip club. Luckily, my step-sister's mom had an immediate opening in the apartment complex she owned. I told her I had no money, but I would get it to her quickly. I was able to move in with no deposit and no first month's rent. I was so thankful that I had a place to live. I made the money quickly and was able to pay all of my bills. I did discover, however, that quick money wasn't easy money.

One night as I was leaving work early in the morning, I got into my hunter green Ford Escort and discovered that something was wrong with one of my tires. The highway was only a few blocks from the club and my tire blew out as I was entering the onramp. I called A. A. A. Within a very short period of time, a tow truck arrived. It didn't say A. A. A., but I figured they must have dispatched it because it was the closest tow truck in the area.

I engaged in small talk with the driver. Then he opened the passenger side door to the tow truck and I got in. He was taking a very long time to hook up my car to his truck. I had free tow miles with A.A.A. and was just going to have my car towed home to deal with the tire in the morning.

I began wondering what was taking so long when a real A. A. A. Tow Truck arrived. The real A. A. A. guy got out of his truck and talked to the man whose truck I was in. Then the A. A. A. driver quickly came to me and yelled through the window, "Ma'am, this man is not a A. A. A.-contracted driver. I don't know who he is. Do you want to come with me?" I sensed that something wasn't right by the intensity in his voice. I looked down at the panel of the passenger side door to open the truck and get out. The door was completely gutted! There was no handle, no way to roll down the window, nothing. I was scared. I told the A. A. A. guy to open the door from the outside because I couldn't get out. He made the guy let me out of the truck.

Thank God that the A.A.A. man showed up when he did! Who knows what would have happened to me? I felt like it was a scene in a horror movie and I had just escaped a gruesome death.

Attempted Suicide

I was extremely depressed and drinking daily. I felt worthless. I met a guy who was visiting home on break from college. He was a friend of some of my friends, a good boy. He knew that I was a stripper and still wanted to be with me. His parents were in ministry and his family was very fun and loving. I think he wanted to save me from myself because he saw that underneath all of my pain and sin, there was someone good deep inside.

One night, I was fighting depression like never before. I was drinking and thinking about my life. I didn't want to live anymore. I made the decision to end my life. I grabbed one of my new butcher knives and began cutting. I wasn't doing this just for attention, but seriously trying to kill myself. There was blood running down my body and all over my apartment. I called my boyfriend to say "bye" to him. It was over. I gave up on myself.

But God didn't give up on me. In that moment, God showed me the same vision He showed me when He explained my calling to me years ago. I saw crowds and multitudes of people hurting, bound, and needing God. I was standing on an outside ministry platform, like a crusade in another country, looking into their lives and ministering freedom, truth, and love. Then I saw myself embracing hopeless, broken, diseased people and they were healed. The Lord gave me a glimpse of what I was born to do. He spoke to my heart as I was drunk, soaked in my own blood, and about to end it all. He said to me, "You can't die. Who will minister to the people I created you to reach?"

I saw another vision of all of the thousands of people in the previous vision lined up in front of me waiting. In that moment, God saved my life again. He didn't let me die. I felt His unexplainable love. He showed me that my life was valuable, I had a purpose, and He needed me. This was the conclusion of a six-month career as a stripper. Almost losing my life was a major shift in my path and journey. My boyfriend wanted me to move with him to Missouri and go to college with him. It was a fresh start, a new life. So I moved from the state of California to the state of Missouri with my boyfriend. Once I got there, I got a job as a phlebotomist in a hospital and enrolled for school full-time. Life was good again; at least for a little while.

Abortion Three

We should not have moved in together, but I enjoyed playing the "wife role," cooking, cleaning, and doing laundry. We went to church together, read our Bibles together. We really tried to keep purity in our relationship. I understood why people at church always said that you shouldn't live together until marriage. We had sex like one and a half times—meaning one of those times, we started and felt convicted, then stopped. I told myself it didn't count since we stopped. Silly me, silly me!

Well, the conclusion was that I got pregnant. He told me that I had to get an abortion, that I couldn't do this to him and that his parents could never find out. He was supposed to be a professional baseball player and there were scouts checking him out at college. He told me that if I had that baby, it would ruin his life. I felt so much pressure and knew that he was forcing me to get an abortion, so I did.

This time was different than the previous two. I felt that I was old enough to try and raise that baby, even if it was going to be hard. I just didn't want my baby growing up without a father like I did. I didn't feel like I had any other option than to just do what he said. He told me that having the baby would ruin his life, but killing the baby ruined mine.

Post-Traumatic Stress Disorder

After the abortion, I found myself in that very familiar place of depression. I had a series of panic attacks and anxiety attacks. The night we came home from the abortion, I cried and screamed for hours. Staring at the wall, I rocked back and forth and screamed, "I want my baby!" Almost immediately after the abortion, my boyfriend went back to the state of California on break. I stayed faithful, paid the bills, kept the apartment clean, and tried to heal from my pain. I started seeing a counselor who diagnosed me with Post-Traumatic Stress Disorder (PTSD).

While my boyfriend was away, our relationship changed. He didn't text or call as much and I knew something was up. I found out he was talking to other girls, so I ended the relationship. I moved into my own apartment and made sure his apartment and car were clean with all bills paid, leaving everything in order for him. I wanted to leave on a good note.

A handsome guy at the gym approached me the same week and asked me if I wanted to hang out sometime. How convenient, I could use him to get over my last relationship. I started talking to him. I had previously resisted his attention at the gym —all of his subtle flirty gestures and smiles—since I wanted to be faithful while I was in a relationship. We started dating and before I knew it, I had jumped into another relationship. I guess focusing on someone else helped me not deal with the hurt I felt from the guy who forced me to get an abortion. This new catch wasn't as beautiful on the inside as he was on the outside. I didn't know that he had drug problems, lying problems, and was mentally "off." I didn't find all of that out until I let him move in with me. He was easy on the eyes and took my mind off of the PTSD I was dealing with. Anything to escape my messed-up reality, right?

The only good thing that came out of this new relationship was that he took me with him one time to Solid Rock Family Church in Jefferson City, Missouri. I was home. This was the church I was searching for the whole time I was in Missouri. This was just what I needed to help me through the anxiety and depression. The presence of God was in that building and the Word the pastor preached always seemed to be about the exact thing that I was dealing with.

Poverty

When I found Solid Rock Family Church, I broke up with the latest boyfriend, moved out, and started really digging deep into God. I let him stay in my old apartment, because I didn't want there to be a reason for him to come back into my space. I took only the bare minimum with me. God was all that I had. I worked part-time at the laboratory and went to school full-time. I only had money to pay my rent and bills with very little left for food. I had no furniture in my new apartment. I slept on the floor with my big comforter, a pillow, and a lamp. That was all I had, aside from a few boxes of books, personal belongings, and a suitcase of clothes.

I walked four miles to school and four miles home. I could only afford to buy oatmeal, ramen noodle soup, and eggs. I remember crying when I went to the store because I was so hungry. There were a few times that I was so embarrassed for others to see my daily container of oatmeal that I ate lunch in the bathroom stall at school. It was hard for me to watch people buying hot dogs, pizza, and sodas. I started dropping a lot of weight and was skinnier than I had ever been. I had too much pride to ask the church to help me and didn't even realize that they would.

Meeting John Mark Skiles

At Solid Rock, I ran every week to the place that I knew wouldn't fail me... the altar. Every time an invitation was made to come forward for prayer, I was there. In fact, that was the first place that John ever really noticed me. He saw me crying and broken on the altar, and through all of my pain, he saw my heart and knew there was something good on the inside. Pastor John was the Worship Leader and the Single's Pastor at the time. He approached me to connect with the singles and college student ministry and we exchanged numbers. When I first met him, I immediately felt a connection and attraction to him. However, I felt so messed up inside that I stopped myself from developing any kind of feelings for him. There was no way that a pastor would ever be interested in me!

We talked on the phone often and started building a really great friendship. Since we laughed a lot together, it was like we had always been friends. One time, we went on a "friend date." We went to see the movie *Santa Clause 2: The Mrs. Clause* and it was horrible, so we left. We drove to his mom and dad's house to hang out for a while. I thought it was so cool that I got to go over to my pastor's house. John's mom decided that she wanted to take a picture of us. Then he took me to his house to show me where he lived and introduced me to his roommate. I remember thinking, wow, I just got a tour of his life all in one night. We had such a fun time hanging out.

Very soon after that, I got scouted out for modeling in Los Angeles by a connection of someone I met last time I was home visiting in California. I told my new BFF John that I was moving back to California. He was disappointed that I was moving. I asked him to take me to the airport shuttle and he did. On the way, he told me that he would have loved to continue getting to know me and possibly date me, if I was staying. I couldn't believe that he actually had some kind of interest in me. Part of me wished that he would have told me sooner. Maybe that would have changed how lonely I was in Jefferson City. I had no idea that the pastor who I was saying goodbye to would later become my husband.

Model/Actress

I was 20 years old and overwhelmed with excitement about being signed to a modeling management company in Los Angeles. I had just moved to L.A. and had immediately started auditioning and doing some small-time modeling and acting work. Modeling wasn't as easy and fun as I thought it would be. I got about one out of every ten auditions that I went to. Auditioning took a lot of time, energy, and sitting in L.A. traffic. I developed an eating disorder during my modeling days. I wasn't skinny enough or tall enough, and had too many curves to get into the magazines and runway shows that I dreamt about, so I ended up in urban men's magazines. Definitely not my dream come true, but I thought maybe that was just the beginning.

I became bulimic and would actually have a panic attack if I was not able to throw up my food quickly enough. I hid this problem from everyone. How surprising... wearing my "safety mask of lies" became my comfort zone yet again. I ended up doing a couple of small roles in movies and found the most pleasure in acting. Acting was an escape from the reality of my painful life, especially during my childhood. I found comfort in it again. I would practice monologues in my room, work on creating characters, and study all of the books and info I could find. I wasn't spectacular on camera, to be honest, but I was a "work in progress." I thought that if I made it in acting, I would use that platform to help people.

I went to auditions during the day and partied all night. Me and my girls loved the VIP treatment. We refused to stand in lines and enjoyed partying in luxury. I actually got paid to be a model hostess at parties and events. We would dance, drink, and laugh all night. We were the pretty comedian girls that were always the life of the party and made everywhere we went a "fun place." In the midst of this, it was really hard to find real friends. Me and my sister/BFF always found ourselves around celebrities and, honestly, didn't see them as anything more than talented people who had excelled in their crafts. We thought asking for autographs and pictures with celebs was just trashy. We would constantly have to weed out friends once we discovered they were groupies and couldn't handle the lifestyle. We never knew who were real friends until time told the truth about them and we had to cut them off. So, we had a lot of fun, but lots of drama, too; there were some crazy situations. There were also some insane stalkers, which came with the territory of being a men's magazine model and a professional drunken partier. When alcohol is part of the daily routine, I guess drama and craziness are inevitable.

Sex Trafficking

One day, I got a call that I was hired for a modeling job in another country. I was told that I would be a model and hostess at an event for a billionaire's clothing line. I had heard of event hostess jobs like that before, so it didn't seem odd to me. In fact, I was extremely excited! I would get to stay at his famous resort and get paid to be a model at an event for his clothing line. I looked up this resort online and big-name celebrities had been there. This was the place that millionaires went for vacation. His clothing line was well known and sold in stores, so everything checked out.

I shared my excitement with my family, that I had an opportunity to spend Christmas in another country! I talked it up so much to my mom and a couple of other family members and friends, because this was "the best modeling job ever!" I was told to be ready for the event upon arrival. I had a one-way ticket, which should have been a red flag.

As soon as I got off of the plane, I changed and touched up my makeup in a bathroom. This was it! I was a world-traveling MODEL! A man in a Hummer picked me up and took me to the resort. When we drove onto the property, I was in disbelief of how beautiful this place was. He took me up to a bedroom and put down my suitcase, telling me this is where I would be staying. He left quickly as I began asking him, "Is this someone else's room?" I saw personal belongings there and it seemed like this room was being lived in. Maybe I was rooming with one of the other models.

Almost instantly, the billionaire came in and I figured out that I was actually in his master bedroom. He greeted me by grabbing my boobs, telling me how sexy I was, and how much fun we were going to have. This shocked me, but I had dealt with perverts before in the entertainment industry. So much was running through my mind. Why did that guy take me to his master bedroom? It must have been a mistake.

I met another girl as we were on our way to this event that I was hired for. She was sweet, but really didn't look like a model to me. When we arrived at the event, there was no red carpet, no marketing material for his clothing line, and no professionals managing or organizing anything. It was just a club. We were escorted in by security to a VIP table. I was so confused and scared. I was trying to put all of the pieces together in my head. I started drinking, something that was already very much a part of my life. I needed a drink, because this whole situation didn't feel right and seemed crazy to me.

The girl I met earlier pulled me in close while the billionaire was socializing. She warned me saying, "Just do whatever he says. Be good. I don't want the same thing to happen to you that happened to the girl they just sent away. She wouldn't have sex with him and he brutally raped her, beat her, and did some really crazy stuff to her sexually. Anal stuff. Just do whatever he says. He is really nice to girls that are 'good.' He says he's going to get my teeth fixed with veneers." Those were not exactly her quoted words, but that's what I remember her saying in that conversation. She also told me to watch what I say on the phones at the resort, "because they listen."

We drove back to the resort after the party was over. I had so much fear inside and didn't know what to do. Here I was, a 20-year-old stupid, stupid girl tricked into flying to another country with a one-way ticket for a "modeling job" and no money to go home. My cell phone didn't work, because I never switched it to an international plan. I couldn't say anything on the phone lines because "they listen." No one had the phone number to the resort to contact me. I felt trapped.

How did this happen? What was he going to do to me? If I was good, he would be nice to me. If I was bad, I would be brutally raped and beaten. I had been raped twice before in my life; I knew what that felt like. So, I opted for option A, "Be good." That night, out of fear, I slept with a monster. The next morning, I went down for breakfast and got a tour of the resort.

I had so many conflicting feelings inside. It was the most beautiful place I had ever seen. White sands, clear water, it looked like paradise.

However, paradise was paired with one of the most despicable sexual encounters I'd ever experienced. It was one more ugly episode to add to the collection of the perverse violations my body endured in life. So, here I was, thinking about horrible things while walking through paradise. I got a massage almost every day. I always kept an alcoholic beverage in my hand, doing anything to keep my mind off of the fact that at any moment he could call me back to the dungeon of his room. I had to stay numb. I couldn't process or understand what had happened to me and how I was going to get home. I told myself over and over, "Just survive, Sula, just survive."

I called my mom and a few others from my room phone line. In my mind, I tried to think about how I could tell them and maybe get a ticket home, but I couldn't say anything on the phone lines; plus, I was so ashamed for getting into this mess. It was easier for me to pretend like nothing happened. I just told them about how beautiful it was there and I wasn't sure when I would be coming home. I don't know why, but I lied. I convinced them that I was spending "Christmas in Paradise."

Every night, more girls showed up for dinner, which was the routine. We all had to dress up and be there promptly on time. Some of the girls were from that country and some from other places. After dinner, he would select the girl of his choice and they had to sleep with him. One night, he called on three of us to come up to his room. The next day, the two girls he selected with me got tickets to fly home. So, I asked the billionaire if I could leave and have a plane ticket, as well. He said, "No," and that I needed to stay because he had someone that I was supposed to meet... his girlfriend. He told me that he purchased me as a Christmas gift for her... WHAT?

So, the pieces of this sick, twisted story came together. I was a young girl purchased as a Christmas gift, lied to, and tricked into coming to another country with the expectation of a modeling job. At that time, I didn't know what sex trafficking was, I didn't know there was actually a name for the evil I was experiencing. I saw many more horrific things during those three weeks held captive, things that were too graphic and painful to even talk about, things that no one should ever have to go through.

I was finally able to convince the girlfriend to get me a ticket home and allow me to leave by telling her that I would continue to be with her. It's crazy how "Stockholm Syndrome & Complex Trauma" work. I told her I just needed to go home and take care of a few things. When I got home, I changed my contact info. Shortly after, I even saw the girlfriend out in the crowd a couple of times at L.A. parties. I was kind to her, but acted like nothing ever happened. I'm not sure if I consciously or subconsciously did this, but the sex trafficking was literally erased from my memory and the trauma was fractured and suppressed until nine years later. I lived for years as if I was never trafficked, completely unaware that it happened to me.

Relationship Flops

After the sex trafficking experience, I returned to the Hollywood party scene. I acted like everything was great and literally erased the previous events from my thoughts. I continued small-time modeling and acting, but I wasn't making enough money to support myself. I got a job as a licensed phlebotomist, drawing blood and doing lab work. I always fell back on the medical field, because it was easy for me to find work since I was nationally certified to do that kind of work.

I ended up in a couple of relationships as I continued

"looking for love in all the wrong places." One of those relationships was full of passion, intensity, and drunken, abusive fights. He was one that I thought I would always be with. Together, we were toxic, a combustive combination. He wasn't faithful to me, but when he was with me, he loved me so much that I overlooked all of the other issues. A bloody swollen lip and a fight there was no turning back from finally sealed the deal on that one.

The next relationship flop was with a prince. I dated him for about a year. I also lived with him and traveled all over the world to Brazil, Paris, Switzerland, Hawaii, and Mexico. He was the most charming man I have ever met. He had a great sense of humor and kept me laughing. I thought I was the only woman in his life and we were hardly ever separated. He spoiled me and took care of me. Unfortunately, behind all of that charm, his huge smile, and frequent words, "I love you," there were many things that I wasn't aware off... including other women. I had to get out of that relationship because, although living like a princess is every little girl's dream, it wasn't a healthy relationship. I made the decision that I would rather be broke, living in a cardboard box alone, than on top of the world with royalty while being cheated on and lied to.

A God Cave

I retreated into what I call a "God Cave." I realized that after living with $30,000 shopping sprees, Gucci, Dolce & Gabbana, butlers, maids, chefs, assistants, security, Bentleys, Maseratis, private planes, and all of the things people dream of, that I wasn't fulfilling my life's purpose. I wasn't doing what I was born to do. I wasn't happy.

I started on a healing and deliverance journey yet again. I spent all day long in my Word, praying, and time in praise and worship. It seemed as though everything that I ever studied or learned of God in my life came back to me. I promised the Lord that I would never run from Him again. I didn't care where His purpose would take me, I would never resist His will again. That was the first time that I made that type of serious commitment to God. I had lived for Him before, preached and taught for Him before. I had prophesied and fasted and praised and worshiped for God before. But never with the determination and dedication of the commitment and decision I just made. I had seen poverty and I had seen royalty. After everything I went through, God became my everything again and the only One worth living for. I said "YES" to the calling on my life. I was done trying to live life for myself.

Marrying into Ministry

The Lord kept putting my old friend, Pastor John Mark Skiles, in my thoughts, so I would pray for him often. Finally, there was a week where I thought about him several times a day, and I knew that I needed to reconnect with him for some reason, but had no idea why. I looked up the church online and called Solid Rock in Jefferson City, Missouri. I left a message on his office phone. He called me back the next day. We were both so excited to reconnect and he said to me, "Sula! You're never going to guess what I found around the same time you called me yesterday... the picture my mom took of us four years ago! It was covered in dust under my bed. I never even knew it was there. Isn't that crazy?" I was shocked and said to God, "Wow, Lord, what are you doin'?" We talked forever and it was like we never missed a day.

Many conversations followed that initial call. We both began recognizing that God was up to something. During one of the calls, John shared his life story with me, including details that he never told any other girl before. He had been raped repeatedly as a little boy by a male family friend and, as a result, had many private struggles and confusion in life. However, God had healed him from that pain. I think he thought that after bearing all to me, maybe I would think of him differently. Something about knowing his story made me love him more. I said to him, "That's nothing, let me tell you my story!" So I did. We shared every dark secret with each other and there was no judgment, condemnation, or negativity.

One day, I was in prayer and felt the Lord overwhelmingly speak to me. He told me that John was the one I was to marry and spend my life with. WOW! I told the Lord that He would have to confirm that to John and that he would have to be the one to say it. I was not going to do what many had done to me before: "The Lord said that I am supposed to marry you!" Ha — they couldn't have been more wrong! I'm so glad I never followed through with empty proposals made to me in the past. This time, God revealed it to me personally so that I wouldn't have to guess. That night, John called me and said, "Don't freak out, but I'm going to marry you one day." I replied by saying, "I know." We both wanted more confirmation and many confirmations did come. God didn't waste any time.

The next day, John went to the public library. A stranger (Hebrews 13:2) approached him and said, "Are you a Christian leader of some sort?" He replied by saying, "Yes." She proceeded to tell him that God sent her there that day to give him a word. She said, "God has showed you the woman you are to marry. Yes, it is her. Don't worry about anything. He will bring her to you. Move forward in faith." The hair on the back of John's neck stood up and he knew that this was yet another undeniable confirmation that really sealed the deal. She disappeared after releasing the word to him. John searched the library for her to thank her. To this day, we're not sure if she was an angel.

Soon after the library event, I flew out to Missouri to visit him for a week and met the rest of his family. I enjoyed attending Solid Rock Family Church again and reconnecting with people. It was so cool to meet the pastoral staff that I would eventually be a part of.

Another interesting moment leading up to our marriage took place on an evening when I was sitting on the couch at my family's house in California. I envisioned having a very simple and intimate backyard wedding with plush greenery and a beautiful elegant set up. Previously, we had only talked about getting married on the beach in Hawaii or someplace like that, but we knew it would be very expensive for family and friends to fly out and attend. Within a few moments of my daydreaming of the simple intimate family wedding, John called me. I could tell he had been crying. And I knew he was speaking from a God-moment he was experiencing. He said, "Don't freak out, but the Lord told me we are not supposed to wait or prolong this wedding. He showed me the date May 25th and I think we are supposed to keep it simple, maybe in my parents' backyard." I knew every word he was saying was the plan we were to follow. He then asked me to marry him officially over the phone. We already knew that was God's plan, but he realized he never officially asked. Of course, I said, "Yes," with tears in my eyes.

We got married about four months after our first reconnection conversation. We have been happily married ever since. Everything about life became brand new and my trauma cycle ended. I'm not saying that everything has been perfect, but I now had a new perspective of how to deal with attacks and adversities. We had each other to live out God's calling and fight for our purposes together.

Happily Ever After

God has healed me, delivered me, and set me free from the trauma, hurt, and pain of my life. Just the fact that I'm alive, completely physically healthy, sane, and happy today is proof that there is a God! There is no human way possible that I could have survived everything in my life all by myself without any help from someone up above. I have no more bipolar disorder, no more PTSD, no more depression, anxiety, or any form of mental illness. I'm excited to wake up every day and live a purpose-filled life. I'm at peace with my past and have forgiven those who've hurt me. I also have healthy relationships with my family. My husband and I love doing full-time ministry together.

One of God's greatest acts of redemption is in the births of our daughter and son who have great purpose on their lives. As church planters, we started a brand-new church in 2014, called "Impact Life Church," in the state of Florida (www.impactlifechurch.us). I also work locally and globally in the rescue and aftercare of trafficking victims as a Survivor Leader & Advocate. Today, I am a speaker, author, minister, and sex trafficking abolitionist! Who would have thought that anything great could ever come out of my life? I enjoy sharing my story to help inspire others, leading them into an intimate love relationship with Jesus. I am proof that a life of pain, sin, and trauma can be transformed into something inspirational.

I'm not saying all of this to brag or be prideful, but to encourage you. No matter what you have been through in life, God has a very special plan for you and you can absolutely be free from everything that has ever kept you bound. If God did it for me, He can't wait to do it for you! So now you're thinking, "Wow, that is an amazing story. How in the world did you get to where you are today?" Let me tell you.

*You will find out in Part Two of this book. It is filled with applicable tools, Scriptures, and information to help you transform your life into one that is free and empowered to live God's purpose for you.

For Part Two of *Fighting for Your Purpose,* order on Amazon or at www.sulaskiles.com.

ABOUT THE AUTHOR

Sula's passion for helping others comes from a painful traumatic life story. She had a childhood of sexual abuse, was institutionalized with a diagnosis of bipolar disorder, has been raped, had issues with drugs and alcohol, had 3 abortions, struggled with bulimia, post-traumatic stress disorder, attempted suicide, anxiety and panic attacks, dysfunctional abusive relationships, she dealt with years of depression and that's just the nutshell version.

In addition Sula was a victim of sex trafficking. She was a young model in Los Angeles who was hired for a modeling job in another country. When she arrived, she found out that it was not at all what she had signed up for. Sula was trapped in a nightmare. She was told a while after arriving that she was actually purchased as a Christmas gift for a billionaire and his girlfriend's sexual pleasure.

Sula has found freedom and healing from the traumas of her life and has been radically transformed through becoming a fiery believer and a follower of Jesus Christ. As a survivor of sex trafficking, she works to spread awareness, teach prevention and help victims and survivors of trafficking. Sula uses her story to help others find the same freedom she has found. It is her joy to advance the Kingdom of God with the love & power of the Gospel. She ministers in faith to see Jesus miraculously heal many. She loves the Presence & Glory of the Lord. Sula invites people into deeper intimacy with Jesus as the Bridegroom King. Jesus performs miracles, signs & wonders through her ministry. Sula is a Pastor, Author and Sex Trafficking Abolitionist. She is happily married to Pastor John Mark Skiles. Together they are Church Planters and started Impact Life Church in Destin, FL March of 2014. They are incredibly blessed to have two beautiful children.

VISIT SULA'S WEBSITE AT:
SULASKILES.COM

SOCIAL:
@SULASKILES

Made in the USA
Columbia, SC
05 July 2020